D0405551

SECOND NATURE:

TALES FROM THE MONTLAKE FILL

BY CONSTANCE SIDLES

Constancy Press, LLC Seattle, Washington

Second Nature: Tales from the Montlake Fill
First Edition

Copyright © 2011 Constancy Press, LLC

Published and distributed by Constancy Press, LLC
4532 48th Avenue NE
Seattle, WA 98105 USA
phone: (206)522-7513
http://www.constancypress.com

Printed in Hong Kong by Mantec Production Company
October 2011

ISBN: 978-0-9842002-1-4 $23.95

Library of Congress Control Number: 2011915560

Dedication and Acknowledgements

Two years ago, when I published *In My Nature: A Birder's Year at the Montlake Fill,* I wrote, "Community is a precious thing. It gives you the chance to share your experiences—your happiness as well as your troubles. It holds you up when you need help. It strengthens each person and multiplies everyone's contributions."

Now that I have finished writing *Second Nature: Tales from the Montlake Fill,* I am more aware than ever of the truth of these observations. Time and again, I turned to a community of caring people for help with my book, and always, always they answered with generosity and kindness. And so I would like to dedicate this book to them:

The photographers who contributed their stunning photos (Tim Kuhn, Doug Parrott, Katie Lloyd, Tom Sanders, Jean Colley, Marc Hoffman, Dennis Paulson, Gregg Thompson, and Loupy Smith); the artists who created their evocative paintings (Molly Hashimoto, Alex MacKenzie, and Penny Bolton); the scientists and citizen-scientists who lent their expertise (Dennis Paulson, Kern Ewing, Katie Messick, Colleen McShane, Herb Curl, Katie Murphy, and Idie Ulsh); the poets and writers who shared their inspirations (Tina Blade, Amy Davis, Alex Sidles, Melinda Bronsdon, and Dianna Moore); the librarians who were always willing to help me track down the information I needed (Martha Ferguson and Rebecca Alexander); my editor (Nick Allison), who found all my malapropisms and bloviations and challenged me—in the kindest possible way—to make my writing better; and most of all my husband John, who birded with me through thick and thin, and who read aloud my stories so we could both hear my words as I always meant them to be: storytelling.

Thank you.

Two Anna's Hummingbirds © Kathrine Lloyd

Contents

Illustrations & Photographs

Artists' and Photographers' Websites

Jean Colley (Friends of Yesler Swamp) ... http://yeslerswamptrail.wordpress.com
Molly Hashimoto . . . . http://www.mollyhashimoto.com
Marc Hoffman . . . . http://dartfrogmedia.com
Tim Kuhn . . . . http://timkuhnphotography.zenfolio.com
Kathrine Lloyd http://9livesimages.com
Alexandra MacKenzie . . . . http://mizmak.blogspot.com

Part I
Winter

1. First Dawn

When I was young, one of my favorite fairy tales was a story about two sisters, a bad-natured girl and a sweet-natured girl. As is common in fairy tales, a witch happened by and decided it would be an interesting sociological experiment to give the two a gift. So she granted the girls a special power that was to last one day. Beginning in the morning, whatever each girl did first, she would continue to do throughout the day.

The evil sister got up at the crack of dawn, intending to sneak into her father's bedroom and filch a pearl from his jewel box. Unfortunately, she stubbed her toe on a slipper she had carelessly left out (she was messy as well as mean). Before she could stop herself, she let out a curse. So she spent the rest of the day stubbing her toe and saying bad words.

The good sister got up and stepped on something cold lying beside her bed. When she bent down to pick it up, she found it was a coin left behind by her messy sibling. So she spent the day bending down and picking up coins. By sunset, she was incredibly wealthy (the witch having to magically supply coins by the dozen, since the evil sister was not in the habit of leaving too much wealth lying around on the floor).

On the theory that folk tales like this persist for centuries because they have a grain of truth at their core, my husband John and I try very hard to find a great first bird on January 1 each year at my favorite place on Earth, the Montlake Fill. The Montlake Fill, known officially as the Union Bay Natural Area, is 75 acres of habitat restored to nature after it closed as a landfill in 1971. It has become one of the premier birding sites in western Washington. Call me superstitious, but I like to think a great first bird at this great birding spot sets the tone for the entire birding year.

One year, for example, we set out for the Fill before dawn to find the Trumpeter Swans that had been driven down to Seattle by the heavy snows of December. A flock of eleven had chosen Union Bay as their winter home-away-from-home. For weeks, they could be seen from many vantage points at the Fill, sailing serenely on the water. As the sun set each night, they would gather in Waterlily Cove for a last dabble of food, and then they would glide into the seclusion of Yesler Cove to sleep. As dawn approached, they would stir and preen, then gradually float out onto the lake. Throughout December, I often found them congregated in the waters near the houses along Surber Drive.

I figured they would be easy to spot as First Bird of the Year. So before dawn on January 1, John and I headed down the Loop Trail to East Point, where we set up our spotting scope. In no time, we saw two large white objects near the water's edge on the far shore. "Score!" my husband cried.

I thought so, too, until I realized the objects weren't moving. Could the swans be asleep? I wondered. But no, not even sleeping swans could be as still as these objects were. "Styrofoam," I said.

You would think large, white swans would stand out like icebergs, even at night, but it was surprising how many pale, swan-like items loomed in the darkness. Upended rowboats on the lawn, folded awnings on the dock, a shed door, a sign, moonlight reflecting on the water, even a goose statue (I think)—all were in danger of becoming First Bird of the Year. Finally, finally, a real swan drifted out of Yesler Cove and took the honor.

True to the fairy tale, that year was a remarkable one for rarities at the Fill. All together, the birding community found 172 different species of birds, a new record. Among them were a bird never before seen at the Fill (a Common Raven) and eighteen species seen fewer than five times in the past 114 years. My favorites: Ash-throated Fly-

Trumpeter Swans © Kathrine Lloyd

catcher (a desert bird), Mountain Bluebird (two females), Northern Saw-whet Owl (christened "The Little Cutie"), and Tennessee Warbler (far from Tennessee).

I loved that year. But as one rarity after another showed up, I began to feel faint regret about my First Bird. It had been such a contrived sighting. John and I had known precisely where to go and what to look for, and thus we had produced the result we wanted. In short, we had controlled the outcome. But the Fill is not, in its essence, a place we humans control. It is a wild place. We may buy it, sell it, plant it, mow it, burn it, or even put trails through it, but we do not truly control it. Nature is what it is, does what it does. No matter how much we humans think we can direct nature, the planet is bigger than we are, older, stronger, more resilient. More wild. Best we remember this, so we remain humble about our powers, grateful for the environment that nurtures us, and careful about our actions.

As that wonder-filled year drew to a close, John and I began to think about the future. New Year's Day was coming up soon, and we had to decide on a strategy. "Maybe we should just go to the Fill at dawn and accept whatever nature sends us," my husband said.

"If we do that, nature is sure to send us a crow," I replied. American Crows are the most widespread bird at the Fill, and I am not fond of them. They're smart but often mean. I guess they remind me too much of ourselves. I'd rather see a swan.

But John's suggestion began to take over my mind. Maybe he was right. The Fill appeals to me because of its wildness, and because it gives me surprises every day. Maybe I should trust it to surprise me on January 1. Nevertheless, I stuck one last oar into the waters of control. "Well, okay, let's go see a crow then," I said a few days later. "But at least let's see crows at their best. Let's go down to the parking lot at the Museum of History and Industry and count crows at Foster Island as they fly toward the Fill before first light. We will see a real phenomenon of nature."

Across the bay from the Fill, Foster Island squats in the lagoons near the 520 floating bridge. For many years, American Crows have come here to roost at night in the wintertime. There is safety in numbers, and crows roost here by the thousands. Just before dawn, they begin to fly out from the island and pass over the Fill, first in threes or fours, then in scores, then in a torrent so dense it is impossible to count them all. By the time the sun peeks over the Cascades, they are gone, only to return again at dusk.

It is a sight well worth seeing, but although he agreed such large numbers of crows would indeed be spectacular, John said even that plan was too contrived.

So on January 1, I found myself in the Fill's Dime Lot with him, waiting for whatever. The weather was dank and cold. Drizzle dotted the windshield. The sun came up but refused to shine through the thick clouds. The birds refused to shine, too. Nothing was moving. My crow phobia began to grow. I feared a crow would show up at any second. At last, I couldn't stand another moment of suspense. "Let's head over to Yesler Swamp," I casually suggested, thinking that Bewick's Wrens are early risers, they love the swamp, and I love wrens. A wren would definitely start the year off right.

My husband gave in and started the car. I guess he wasn't that crazy about crows in single digits either. In the swamp, all was quiet except for the drip drip drip of water off the eaves of my increasingly floppy hat. We sat in the swamp for long minutes with nothing to show for our pains except sogginess. I sighed. "There's nothing here," I said, stating the obvious.

My husband nodded, and we began to splash our way back to the car, John in the lead. At the edge of the trees he halted so abruptly I bumped into him. "Don't look!" he shouted.

But it was too late. A crow was sitting on the wire above our car, looking right at us. My beady eyes met its beady eyes. Then the crow threw back its head and cawed its raucous laugh. I looked sourly at John. Great.

That night as I recorded my sightings for the day, I reflected on the meaning of American Crow as First Bird. Homilies and adages ran through my mind: Bloom where you're planted. If life gives you lemons, make lemonade. Every day is a special day. We live in a golden age when the ordinary can be extraordinary.

Nothing helped. I felt like the ugly sister who had stubbed her toe and now could look forward to nothing but curses. Why keep trying when you've already lost? I sank deeper into my self-made pit. More negative thoughts began to crowd in. Birding is not the only thing I care about at the Fill. I also care deeply about preserving the habitat so the wild can continue to thrive here. Yet recent events have made me realize how difficult preserving even a measly 75 acres can be. The University of Washington is experiencing the Great Recession now. The state legislature, which should be responsible for funding this incredible engine of education, job growth, and innovation, has closed its wallet. The governor told the faculty to brace for another cut. Rumor has it this one will be 10 percent, added to other cuts made over the last couple years.

In response, the Center for Urban Horticulture caretakers, who try their best to be good stewards of this site, have elected to turn one of the prairie fields into a temporary parking lot. It is not the birdiest of the prairies. Nobody breeds in the tall grasses, as far as I know. But the Bald Eagles come here to rip up grass with their talons so they can line their nest nearby with softness. Western Kingbirds stop here during migration to hunt for insects. Savannah Sparrows perch on the raised beds and cry their buzzy cries in the summer. The Alder Grove bordering the west side of this field is the best place to look for warblers and vireos in the spring, Brown Creepers in the winter, and wrens all the time.

I hate to see this habitat degraded by cars and oil leaks, but I cannot guarantee to raise thousands of dollars every year to replace lost parking fees. Maybe it's necessary to sacrifice a small field to save the larger whole, and I should let it go. Jane Goodall, the world-famous chimpanzee zoologist, has been working all her adult life to save her precious chimps of the Gombe Reserve in Africa, but despite all her efforts, the chimpanzee population has shrunk to under 100 individuals. If Jane Goodall can't save the planet, I mused, then who can? I could feel myself spiral lower.

"Gonna hit bottom any time now," I told myself. But before the big ker-splash, I heard another sound. It was the soft screech of socks

American Crow © Kathrine Lloyd

getting stretched as I hauled myself up by them. "Well, this is a fine howdy-dee-doo," I lectured myself. "One little crow and you think the whole rest of the year is shot. One little setback and you think all is lost. Where the heck is your spine?"

At my age, my spine is always with me, sending me constant messages about how human evolution has failed to produce a back that works without aching. However, since at heart I am still a lithesome eighteen, I rarely pay any attention to such bodily signals. I straightened up. My spine got happier. No setback was going to intimidate me!

It is so easy to get discouraged when the world hands you a crow instead of the graceful swan you really wanted. Keeping up your spirits at such times can seem to be an impossible task. But we are all stronger than we think we are, more capable of building something up instead of tearing something down, better at kindness, more courageous.

When my oldest son Alex went to boot camp to become a Marine, he told me about an exercise the drill instructor required all the men to perform. "They call it building a house," he said. "We get down on our bellies, then we raise our butts as high as we can to make a triangle shape, holding ourselves up with our toes and our fingers."

"That doesn't sound so hard," I replied.

"It isn't—for the first hour or two. But after that, it gets very hard!" he laughed. "There was one guy who collapsed after a while. The sergeant ran up to him and started yelling, 'Get up! Get up! Get up!' But the kid said he was too exhausted. 'I just can't do it anymore, sir,' he said. The sergeant kept yelling at him until finally the kid got up and built himself into a house again. I learned a big lesson from that."

"What was the lesson?" I asked, thinking maybe it had something to do with fear as a motivator.

"That you can do more than you think you can," said Alex, with deeper wisdom than mine. "That kid was sure he couldn't get up again, but he could. And he did."

We can, too.

Male Spotted Towhee © Kathrine Lloyd

2. Secret Swamp

If the demigod Pan ever hops a plane for Seattle, I know the first place he will visit. It will be the hidden grove east of the greenhouses and west of Surber Drive, where the birds live their secret lives undisturbed by city folk. This is Yesler Swamp.

If you want to enter Pan's wild kingdom, you will have to find the twisty path that snakes down from the parking lot, past the cane bushes where the Fox Sparrow prowls. You must tread this path silently to avoid detection, but it won't be easy. The gateway is guarded by a Spotted Towhee, who mews his "all-clear" to every denizen of the grove. His call sounds like a kitten crying for its mother, but the other birds are not fooled. They know he's no lost baby, helpless and alone. When he falls silent and retreats into hiding, they accept his assessment of danger and disappear, too.

There is no way to placate the sentinel, no offering you can make to win acceptance. If you time it right, though, you can catch him when he's busy singing a different tune, a dry rattle that sounds like someone shaking a rain-tube toy. It is his territorial song, designed to scare off rivals. When he sings it, he throws his head back, fixes his eyes on the sky above, and gives it everything he's got. While the towhee is absorbed making his big impression, you can sneak by unnoticed. Be careful not to step on any twigs or brush against any leaves. Tiptoe slowly down the trail until you come to a break in the dense bushes. Before you, the grove opens up, ringed with trees and encircled by fingers of lake water.

Winter is the best season to come to this part of the swamp. The weeds that choke the path in the depths of summer have all died back, and the mosquitoes who think of me as their meal ticket to reproductive heaven have not yet hatched.

One January day, I was walking around the Loop Trail at the Fill, trying to decide if I had the energy to hike to the swamp and outwit the guardian towhee. Ordinarily, this kind of decision would be a no-brainer, but January has been unusually cold this year, and I could feel my core temperature dropping into the single digits. I found myself thinking about the wall heater in my living room that bakes my toes when I put my feet up on the windowsill. I began to hear a pot of hot chocolate calling to me, and the call was a lot louder than any of the chirps of the few hardy birds out braving the cold. Chirps were doing nothing for me. Not even the tootles of the Trumpeter Swans floating majestically on the bay could divert my mind from hot chocolate. I turned toward the parking lot and home but soon ran into two birder friends. They told me they had just been inside Yesler Swamp and had found a Brown Creeper.

Brown Creepers are little tree-climbers arrayed with natty brown-and-white checks on their backs and spanking-white cravats at their throats. They hunt for tiny insects and spiders by flying to the base of a tree, then they brace themselves against the trunk with their stiff tails. They look like mini-woodpeckers, but this is deceptive. Woodpeckers brace themselves in order to hammer holes into a tree so they can poke in their incredibly long, sticky tongues to snag insects. Creepers don't hammer anything. Instead, they probe the bark with their long, pointed bills as they hitch themselves upward in a spiral, around and around the tree trunk.

Brown Creepers are one of my favorite birds. Any day I see one is a good day. I'd been trying to find one for weeks, to no avail. I knew creepers were in the swamp because I'd often heard their high-pitched songs, but no matter how many times I went, I could never see them. "That does it," I told my friends. "I'm going to go over there and sit on my camp stool until I see one, even if it takes until March."

I have often thought how lovely it would be to go to the Fill and never come back to any other reality. No need to punch the time clock, no family train wrecks to put back on the rails, no yard to weed. There's an unoccupied pole that sticks up in the marsh. Pole saints in the Middle Ages would have found it more than adequate, and why shouldn't I, too? The Laurelhurst neighbors might object, and there's probably some kind of city ordinance against permanent loitering on a pole, but it is still tempting. Imagine experiencing the seasons as they spin by, heralded by the comings of some birds and the goings of others.

With all thought of hot chocolate and warm heaters banished, I arrived at the trailhead and immediately stepped on a stick, which snapped with the sound of a howitzer firing a round. The guardian towhee gave one frightened squawk and dove into the bushes, never to emerge. So did every other bird.

Undaunted by this misstep, I set up my camp stool and waited. Usually, if the birds of the swamp have been disturbed, it takes 20 minutes or more of silence before they venture forth again. Ordinarily, I don't wait that long for anyone, even a bird, but since I had made up my mind to sit here until March, mere minutes had lost all meaning. Time passed, but how much time I had no idea.

Eventually, the birds calmed down, and the swamp came back to life. Black-capped Chickadees flew by, then hung upside down on twigs to forage for insects. Dark-eyed Juncos flashed their white tail feathers as they flitted among the winter weeds. Two Ruby-crowned Kinglets fed almost at my feet, and a Song Sparrow came out to dig through the leaf litter, scattering bits of leaf far and wide.

Then three Steller's Jays popped out of nowhere, calling raucously. They were remarkably difficult to see as they hopped from bush to bush. You'd think their blue feathers would make them stand out from the browns and beiges of the winter foliage, but no. I suppose part of their ability to disappear in full view is due to their intelligence: Steller's Jays take every advantage of shade and cover to hide, seeming to know exactly how to make their dark-gray heads, crests, and backs blend in with the dark colors of shaded forest. But part of their ability to disappear is also due to the fact that their blue feathers are not really blue at all. Rather than blue pigment, the feathers are filled with tiny air pockets that scatter light. Because blue light has a short wavelength, it scatters more than the other wavelengths when it hits molecules of air. That is why our sky is blue, and it is also why Steller's Jays are blue. Mixed in with the air pockets of a jay's feathers are melanin granules that absorb all the wavelengths of light. The combination of melanin granules and air pockets produces a dark blue that looks even darker when the feathers are in shadow. If you know where to look for a jay, you can pick it out of the shadows because it will always look bluer to your eyes than the other colors of the forest; but if you aren't sure exactly where the jay is, your eyes might easily slide right over it, as its gray feathers and dulled blue blend in with the surrounding shade.

Pondering these mysteries of light and dark, I began to take the time to notice other things I often miss: the way a slight breeze lifted a few feathers under a chickadee's throat, the glitter of a Song Sparrow's bright shoe-button eyes, the foraging technique of a Bewick's Wren who exuberantly flung aside a leaf in its search for a spider. I heard two Pacific Wrens singing very softly nearby but did not see them. No matter. March was still some weeks away, and I knew the wrens were bound to come out into the open at some point.

In the meantime, a Cooper's Hawk flew in, perched in a cottonwood tree, let out a melodious screech (if screeches can be so described), and was joined by a second Cooper's. I think they are a pair; perhaps they will make more hawks this season.

Then I heard a quiet pinprick nearby. I looked in time to see a tiny body with a stiff tail creep behind a tree trunk and then emerge briefly to give me a perfect view. Ah, Brown Creeper at last. It began to ascend the tree, hitching itself along like a miniature funicular. It chugged halfway up the tree, then with a flick of its tail, like a magician waving his wand in the final act, the bird disappeared. I thought for a second that I saw a puff of smoke where the creeper had been, but it was just my breath curling into steam.

I was smiling as I folded up my camp stool and tiptoed away. Back to the cold and to reality, yes, but I know the swamp and its magic will be here waiting for me, always.

Brown Creeper © Doug Parrott

3. Counting Gulls

You can always tell when a winter storm pounds the Puget Sound coast—gulls by the thousands are driven far inland to escape the wind and the tides. Many of them settle on the playfields north of Clark Road. Here they march, march, march in platoons across the grass, stopping every few steps to pull a worm out of the ground.

I think most of the worms they get are night crawlers. I say this because the worms seem reluctant to let go of the earth, and they're surprisingly strong. They grip tenaciously, as if their lives depended on it, which of course they do. I've often seen a big gull pulling on a worm that stretches and stretches elastically until it's almost ten inches long. Of all the worms that live in western Washington, only night crawlers can stretch this far. Finally the worm lets go and snaps into the gull's bill like a boy shooting off a rubber band. Whap.

Night crawlers are not native worms. They were brought here from Europe to the East Coast, some say by farmers, others say by fisherfolk. They spread rapidly, considering they are just worms. Now they fill the earth from one end of the continent to the other.

Unlike our native worms, which crawl horizontally through the earth, taking in dirt at one end and excreting fertilizer from the other, night crawlers burrow vertically. They dig a tunnel down into the earth as deep as twelve feet. They're safe down there, but they can't find enough to eat, so every night they crawl up to the surface to feed. If the ground becomes too wet and their burrows get saturated with water or with collapsed soil, the night crawlers stay near or at the surface. That's when the gulls come.

I've often marveled at how many worms there must be in the dirt of the playfield. This past January has been a wet month, and the gulls have come here every single day. I have counted up to 150 birds at once, all pulling out worms at the rate of one every 20 seconds or so. On a good day, that's 450 worms a minute, or 27,000 an hour. Fortunately for the worms, the gulls can't keep up this pace all day. By midmorning, the gulls are forced to leave because the college kids wake up and come out to play Ultimate Frisbee or soccer. Most days, the gulls have the field to themselves for only two hours in the morning. But that still means they're nabbing 54,000 worms every day. Three hundred seventy-eight thousand a week. One and a half million a month.

You'd think the gulls would soon exhaust the food source, but night crawlers are indefatigable breeders. They can hatch a brood of up to 20 babies every two weeks. I doubt they ever rest. Normally, worms need moist conditions to breed, and they can take a break when it's dry. But the playfield is irrigated throughout the summer, making year-round breeding possible. Talk about exhausting.

Most of the gulls who come to the playfield in winter belong to only three species: Mew Gull, Ring-billed, and Glaucous-winged. All these species are abundant in Seattle in the winter, and they all like worms. Occasionally, a California Gull shows up, or a Herring or Thayer's Gull. In fact, this very playfield is one of the best places to compare different gulls with each other and drive yourself crazy trying to figure out which is which.

A lot of birders don't even try, but I have found if you work at it, you can usually tell. Three species have yellow legs, and four have pink. Some have light eyes and others dark, though you have to be careful on gray days, when all the gulls' pupils get big and dark. Most gulls have black-tipped wings. Only the Glaucous-winged has gray-tipped wings, but unfortunately for the birder, these gulls frequently hybridize with black-tipped ones, and the resulting babies come out with dark-gray tips. Trying to decide whether a gull's wing is tipped with black or just very dark gray is one of the greatest pleasures and puzzles of the gull identification game.

Mew Gull © Tim Kuhn

To me, an even greater puzzle is why there are so many different species at all. When they visit the Fill, the gulls mix together, and they all do the same things. They roost on the same roof-tops, forage for the same worms, fly to the same lake to bathe and drink, and peck at the same garbage the morning after a football Saturday.

What possible evolutionary pressure could have produced so many different species when you'd think nature wouldn't have to bother with more than one or two?

The answer, I guess, is hard for us to figure out because we don't see gulls at their best. Except for the highly pelagic species such as Sabine's, gulls don't live in their native habitats anymore. Humans have altered the landscape too dramatically. Gulls are all opportunistic feeders, and when people came along to make more of a smorgasbord for them, the gulls dug right in. They may have eaten a health-nutty diet of raw fish and eggs when they had nature to themselves, but now the gulls have added fast food, table scraps, and tailgate snacks to their diet. They still catch a few fish, and of course they take their worms tartare. But there's no doubt that gulls are becoming more like us every day, at least foody-wise.

Perhaps that's why people have lost respect for them. Gulls don't seem wild anymore. They eat a lot of garbage, so they have become garbage birds. You are what you eat, after all. Even birders usually dismiss them when they see them soaring by. "Oh, that's just a gull," the birders will say, with few exceptions.

Nonbirders are even more dismissive. One man comes nearly every morning to the playfield to exercise his greyhound. He does this by siccing the dog onto the platoons of marching gulls. The dog races around like a lightning bolt, chasing first one platoon and then another until all the gulls have been frightened into the sky, where they wheel around crying forlornly for their lost worms. The man laughs, and so does the dog. What fun.

This scenario invariably makes me think of Annie Proulx's story "The Hellhole," published in her book of short stories *Bad Dirt*. "Hellhole" is the story of a Wyoming Game and Fish warden, Creel Zmundzinski, whose job it is to catch poachers. One day, Zmundzinski finds a minister who has illegally shot a mother moose, leaving an orphaned calf behind to face death, too. In the course of forcing the minister to pack out his kill, Zmundzinski endures the minister's threats, name-calling, and whiny excuses. Back at the parking lot, as he writes out a ticket for the potty-mouthed poacher, Zmundzinski notices that the minister is standing on a circle in the gravel. When the minister stamps his foot and jumps up and down in rage, "there was a sound like someone tearing a head of lettuce apart. The gravel heaved and abruptly gaped open. The hunter dropped down into a fiery tube about three feet across that resembled an enormous blowtorch-heated pipe. With a shriek the preacher disappeared."

All that's left, writes Proulx, is a sooty circle and the faint smell of sulfur.

Zmundzinski is stunned by this event, of course, but also pleased. He tells the other wardens about the hellhole, and they start bringing unpleasant park attendees to the parking lot, too. Once there, the wardens get the malefactors to stand in the circle and stamp, and poof! down go the delinquents, never to offend again.

I have seen such a circle in the Dime Lot. I had thought it was the result of the frat boys making donuts with their muscle cars. I had also thought that the faint smell of rotting eggs I have occasionally caught was just a whiff of the garbage decaying in the landfill, or perhaps the porta-potties that appear on football Saturdays for the sake of the fans who drink too much beer. But now I'm not so sure. I've begun to wonder how to entice that dog owner to race his greyhound around in the Dime Lot. Could I get him to stand in the middle of the donut-shaped depression and jump up and down?

This may seem mean-spirited to you, and I guess it is. But Greyhound Man enrages me. Clearly, he loves animals. After all, he probably adopted a racing dog that would otherwise have been euthanized by hard-hearted dog breeders once its racing life had passed. So how can a person who loves animals be so cruel to gulls? Not that chasing the birds hurts them very much. They are so quick to flush and fly when the dog shows up that there is no chance the dog will ever catch them.

On the other hand, the gulls struggle to make a living. They have to forage every day against strong competition. If they miss a day of worms, they must struggle that much harder or die. They don't have a warm, dry house to go back to at the end of the day. They can't call for takeout if they don't feel up to foraging.

It's true that gulls are very common in Seattle. They aren't endangered. So why should we care what happens to a few of them?

I say we should care because they are fellow creatures with their own lives to lead, just as we are. A gull is not a person, that epitome of all creation, but it is a living being. Furthermore, unlike the man and his greyhound, gulls belong here. They're natives. And we humans have already deprived gulls of so much of their native habitat. Must we chase them as well? Wouldn't it be better for us to demonstrate kindness and compassion for gulls just because they exist here with us?

More than that, though, gulls deserve our care because they are a symbol of the wildness of the Pacific Northwest. I remember walking the beaches of Whidbey Island as a girl and hearing their wild and lonely sounding cries. Now that I'm older, there is nothing in nature that speaks to me of the wild more clearly than do gulls. When I hear them, they remind me that I, too, am wild and sometimes lonely.

We need to be reminded of such things, for wildness is the well-spring of originality, and loneliness of creativity. Wildness is the opposite of conformity. When we are wild, we experience the uniqueness that we each hold within ourselves. When we are lonely, we can think our own thoughts, untrammeled by the views and expressions of others.

I used to tell my middle-school writing students that they were special. Not in the pap-filled way that adults often employ. Far from it. I was being scientifically accurate. Each of us is special, I would argue, because we are each unique. No one else on the planet has the specific combination of DNA and experience that work together to set us apart from all others. Not even identical twins are the same. They share the same DNA, but each one has different experiences in life, and so each one becomes separate. You can't make a copy.

Furthermore, no one else in the whole history of the planet has ever been our duplicate. In fact, no one in the future ever will be, no matter how many billions of us occupy the Earth.

That means when we create something from within ourselves—a painting, a story, a song, a child—it, too, is unique. Most important of all, if we decide not to create that work, then no one else ever will. No one else can. And thus the world will be forever deprived of the splendor it might have had.

So the next time you see a gull in the wild—or even in the not-so-wild, when it's pulling worms out of a playfield or fries out of a McDonald's bag—I ask you to stop, look, and listen. Perhaps the gull will give its wild and lonely cry, and you will feel wild and lonely, too. Wild enough to feel free. Alone enough to feel unique. And you will know that the world needs you to give back to it what you alone can give. Yourself.

Glaucous-winged Gull © Thomas Sanders

4. It's a Bird

I found out today that I have a secret identity. I was sitting on my camp stool on Surber Drive, gazing into Yesler Swamp below as I vainly attempted to see one of my favorite but most elusive birds, the Pacific Wren. A couple out walking in the early-morning frost stopped to look into the grove with me. All three of us stared, riveted, but nothing was moving. We might as well have been staring at a painting on the wall. The minutes ticked by. No one said a word. Finally, judging that enough time had passed in this silent reverie, the woman said, "I simply must ask you your name. We see you sitting here so often with your binoculars that we've wondered who you really are. We call you the Bird Lady."

I was taken aback. A person could interpret a remark like that in many ways. On the one hand, it could mean that you're the crazy old woman with hair sticking out in raggedy tufts who walks around town talking to herself. I do talk to myself, and on humid days, my hair frizzes up like raggedy tufts of froth on a double-tall latte.

On the other hand, it could mean that you're the lovable neighborhood character whom everybody recognizes, nobody really knows, but everyone would miss if you weren't in your accustomed place at the usual time. "Oh, yeah, that's the Bird Lady. She comes here every day at dawn. Hi there, Bird Lady."

Or it could mean that you're a superhero with unearthly powers. "Faster than a speeding Merlin. More powerful than a Bald Eagle trying to drag a heavy salmon out of the water but incapable of doing so because the salmon is just too big. Able to leap small puddles in a single bound. Look! Up on her camp stool. It's a bird. It's a plane. It's Bird Lady!!!! Yes, it's Bird Lady, strange visitor from another planet, who came to the Fill with 10-power binoculars far beyond those of mortal men; Bird Lady, who can change course at the sight of any new bird; bend blackberry brambles with her bare hands; and who, disguised as Connie Sidles, mild-mannered writer for whomever will give her an assignment and send her a check in the mail, fights a never-ending battle for truth, justice, and the environmental way."

I could join the real-life superheroes featured on the World Super-hero Registry website. These are people from all over the world who get dressed up in a costume of "sufficient quality to show some care went into its creation," as the website says. To be listed in this official registry, you have to commit to do your best to make the world a better place.

My two favorite real-life superheroes are Angle Grinder Man and Red Arrow. Angle Grinder Man is a British guy who "patrols the night looking for unhappy drivers who have been clamped, and then sets their cars free." Red Arrow is a Hong Kong guy who wears a stuffed red arrow on his head and an appliquéd red arrow on his blue chest. His head arrow points up, and his chest arrow points down. This caped crusader tries to "bring happiness to people and become the salt and light of the world." Salt and light are not the first two things I would normally come up with if I had to describe the essential ingredients of do-goodness, but really, what would our planet be like without them?

After these thoughts had run a couple of laps around the race-track of my mind, I came to and told the neighbor woman and her husband my name. Inquiring minds want to know, and the Lau-relhurst neighbors like to be assured that you're not going to do anything too weird. At least, not anything weirder than trying to watch birds on days so cold you can't feel your toes anymore as you wait in vain for the birds to show themselves. I've certainly done that many times. I guess my secret superhuman power must be indefatigable sitzfleisch.

Although I'm still of two minds about whether I should be flattered or insulted about my neighborhood identity, I must admit there is one thing I like about being Bird Lady, and that is the manner in which I assumed my superheroism. Contrary to so many of the comic books I read as a youngster, I didn't have to be bitten by a radioactive spider, launched in a rocket by my parents to escape a dying planet, or bequeathed a magic green ring. I acquired my superhero identity in the most ordinary way: I took walks in nature.

It's the ordinariness of my experience that I think matters, because it means that we can all be superheroes. In fact, maybe we are, at least now and then.

In Jewish mystical tradition, it is said that there are 36 righteous people alive in the world for whose sake God will preserve us all. They are called Lamed-Vav Tzaddikim (or Lamed-Vavniks for short), the Hebrew/Yiddish phrase for "36 Righteous Ones."

No one knows who the Lamed-Vavniks are. Even the Lamed-Vavniks themselves do not always know. You can guess their identity because they are humble, saintly people who bend all their efforts to help others, but you can't know for sure whether you're right.

This secret identity is key to their success: Since no one knows who the Lamed-Vavniks are, we must all assume that any one of us *could* be one. As such, we have a duty to help others whenever we can and live humbly ourselves. The fate of the world may very well rest in our hands.

We all know people who could be one of the 36. I have a feeling that several of them got together when the Montlake Landfill closed forever in 1971. At that moment in history, the University of Washington had to decide what to do with the new land created by the endless parade of garbage trucks that had been busily turning wetlands into flat land since 1926, the year the University leased the first parcel of marsh to the City of Seattle.

I've seen photos of what the landscape looked like back then. It was a vast, open area of smoothed-over dirt, bisected by a couple of polluted sloughs, with a few scraggly bushes scattered here and there, and the odd pond. Few people would have been able to look at that desolation and envision the glorious place it is today, a haven used by more than 240 different species of birds. Yet the visionaries who set this land aside and the ones who managed to preserve it as a natural area down through the years were somehow able to look into the future, and they made that future a reality.

In the truest Jewish tradition, I won't name these superheroes, but I will acknowledge the great debt we owe to them. Because of what they did, we have a precious bit of the wild in the heart of our city, where all of us can go to renew our connection to nature.

As I sat near Yesler Swamp, contemplating the work of these secret heroes, a tiny Pacific Wren ventured out onto a bare tree limb. With a quick glance at me, to make sure I wasn't going to pounce and eat him, he took a deep breath, fanned out his tail as wide as it could go, threw back his head, and trilled an aria that filled the entire grove.

On July 7, 1990, José Carreras, Plácido Domingo, and Luciano Pavarotti stepped onto the stage at the Baths of Caracalla in Rome and began a concert that has become a legend in the opera world. Ostensibly, the concert was in honor of the World Cup in soccer, but really the concert was a celebration of Carreras's victory over cancer.

As the three opera greats each took his turn, I noticed that Carreras seemed to throw himself into his part much more thoroughly than the other two. He was by far the smallest singer of the three, and I suspect he wanted his voice to sound as big as theirs. To achieve this volume, he literally filled himself with air, stood up on his toes, and quivered.

The Pacific Wren reminded me of him. It is the smallest of our wrens, and it must compete against its larger colleagues in order to claim its share of territory and attract a mate. Like Carreras, this wren filled himself with air, stood on his toes, quivered his wings, and gave a performance worthy of the best that Domingo or Pavarotti ever achieved. His music was celestial, ethereal. It filled the grove the way a great tenor can fill a cathedral. As he sang, a little bank of fog drifted into the grove and was snagged by the bare fingers of the willows. Slowly, the fog floated down until a misty veil covered

Pacific Wren © Dennis Paulson

the singer. Still he sang, his music now bodiless, timeless. Finally the last note quivered from within the clouds, hovered momentarily over the grove, then faded away.

No words can thank the wren for such beauty, nor can I think of any that would suffice to thank the people who made such an experience possible. The gift is too superhuman for that.

5. Teals and Technology

The male Green-winged Teals have been working on their feathers all winter, and today, the first of February, they were ready to do battle for the attention of their fair females. Who, I'm sorry to say, paid no attention to them whatsoever.

Green-winged Teals are not nature's most fearsome warriors. They are among the smallest of our state's ducks, and perhaps the mildest. They are lovers, not fighters. When other ducks put their heads down flat on the water and paddle furiously toward each other, like aqueous jousters tilting in a medieval tournament, the Green-winged Teals sit on the sidelines and chirp. Oh, they'll give each other an occasional nip when they're feeling irritated enough, but you can tell their hearts aren't really in it.

However, even Green-winged Teals feel the hormones begin to flow in late winter, and they are moved to duel. I watched six males displaying their prowess on the Lagoon today. You have to have quick eyes to see how they scrap because their clashes are over in less than two seconds. Green-winged Teals always give me the impression they'd rather be reciting poetry.

Here's a typical exchange. One male paddled close to another and fluffed out the feathers of his dark green mask. Then the male formed his green neck feathers into a discrete point at the back and quickly raised his neck up and ratcheted it back down again, like a Pez dispenser granting a small candy. The display ended with a little chirp. "Take that, you varlet."

The second male, not to be outdone, pointed his little feathers into a crest, ratcheted his neck up and down, and gave his own little chirp. "How do you like them apples, buster?"

This excited the other males so much that they all pointed their crests and ratcheted their necks at each other. A big chirp-fest ensued. The females went to sleep.

I sometimes think that when Adam and Eve goofed up on their food groups, causing mass expulsions from the Garden of Eden, Green-winged Teals avoided the eviction orders and stayed behind to dabble in the perfect pools and lagoons of paradise. When they finally decided to join the rest of us in the real world, Green-winged Teals brought with them a whiff of that ancient Eden, a place where peace reigned, where the lion lay down with the lamb and refrained from eating lamb chops, where everyone got along, and there was abundance for all.

Green-winged Teals grace the lagoons and ponds of our local paradise now. I've seen them at the Fill every month except June. I can often find them on a lazy winter's day, floating half-asleep on the water, letting the slow current take them where it will. It's easy, when I watch them, to let my cares float away on the current along with the ducks. They look so content and peaceful.

But looks can deceive. Nature is not really peaceful, at least not very often and not for very long. The teals may not war with each other, but they sometimes become casualties just the same: the victims of their predators, the falcons and bird-eating hawks that are as much a part of nature as are the teals.

We may love nature, but let us never forget that nature does not love us back. Nature cannot love or hate. It is literally heartless, meaning it has no heart. It won't listen to appeals for mercy, it can't take pity on the weak, it doesn't forgive stupidity, nor does it respond to prayers or payments. In short, nature doesn't care about us one way or the other, and that is why we must always respect its power.

I remember one time my family and I had hiked to the end of Hawai'i Volcanoes National Park to see the lava flowing out of Kilauea. The lava was oozing down the mountainside over the road

Male Green-winged Teal © Kathrine Lloyd

and into the sea. The eruption was slow-moving, so slow that a gray crust had formed over the lava, making it look solid. You could tell the lava wasn't solid, though, because you could hear it creak as it moved slowly over the road. Occasionally, a short crack would open up in the gray crust, and the red eye of the lava would leer out.

The lava flow was open to tourists, and many of us had hiked a mile to see it. One woman wanted her picture taken to show that she had been there, done that. She walked out onto a little overhang that was suspended a few inches above the lava. "Take my picture, dear," she cooed to her husband, backing up on the overhang.

Nearby, a park ranger stood and watched. I thought the woman was foolhardy in the extreme. What was to keep the little overhang from breaking under her weight and spilling her into the lava? What safety mechanism was in place to keep her from backing right off her perch? "Aren't you going to do anything?" I asked the ranger.

"I've told her," he said grimly. His attitude—a very western one—was that it was not his responsibility to correct stupidity.

Fortunately, the husband snapped the picture quickly, and the foolish woman strode back to safety. No harm done. In fact, I'm sure the woman thought there had been no peril at all. Like the rides at Disneyland, nature for her presented only illusory risk, scary enough to make her experience fun but not really dangerous.

I suppose this desire to believe our environment is safe is the real reason humans invented civilization. It doesn't take too many lion attacks before you realize raw nature is something you'd better protect yourself from. Even before *Homo* became *sapiens,* we needed a buffer between us and nature. No fur? Make a jacket. No fangs? Make a spear point. No rumen? Make fire and invent haute cuisine.

Since those early days in our prehistory, we have lived in two worlds: the natural world, and the created one. And as anyone who has lived in two different worlds will tell you, it can be difficult to reconcile them.

The 21st-century way of reconciliation seems to be to fool ourselves into believing that we can control nature by increasing and refining technology. If only we had more gadgets, we would be fine, we tell ourselves. No need to alter our dependence on cars—we just have to invent a car that runs on water or cornstarch or some other green thing. Global climate change? We don't have to change our ways. All we have to do is invent little heat-absorbing gadgets, shoot them into the atmosphere, and let them orbit us to sustainability. Too little food for the growing billions? Let's invent a new Green Revolution. Overfishing our salmon and cod and dolphins and dozens of other species? Hi-tech fish farms are the answer. Hi-tech is always the answer.

I'm as much a believer in Technology as anyone. Maybe more so because I have so little understanding of how it really works. In fact, I am constantly astounding my physics-trained husband with the depth of my unfounded beliefs. One day I was spouting off about how technology can do anything. "Just because we haven't yet invented a good way to solar-power our Civic doesn't mean we can't," I said. "Someone in the near future will find a way. We're so ingenious that eventually we will always find a way."

"Not every problem has a technical solution," my husband said.

"All righty then," I responded, "name a problem that cannot be solved technically."

I thought I had him, until he came back with: "Build a car out of balsa wood."

I suppose you could say that technically, my husband won that argument. But in reality, we both won, for I do not truly wish to believe that technology will endlessly sustain constant growth in human populations and material gains. Someday, as a species, we will have to create a balance between our two environments, the natural and the cultural.

I was interviewed last year by KUOW's reporter Jeannie Yandel. She wanted to walk around the Fill with me and talk about birding. One of her first questions was, "How often do you come out here?"

"Nearly every day," I replied.

Jeannie could not believe her ears. "Every day?" she kept asking over and over.

I tried to explain why this was not weird. "The Fill is different every day," I said. Blank look.

"Different birds come here in different seasons." Wrinkled brow of puzzlement.

"It's fun to get to know one place intimately." Nope.

Ever since that interview, I've been trying to come up with an explanation that makes sense to people. I suppose, given my commitment to the environment, I could say coming to the Fill every day requires 1.8 miles of driving for me, whereas going to a different place each time I want to bird would use up far more gasoline and produce far more pollution.

While true, this isn't why I spend part of every day at the Fill, if I can possibly manage it. The real reason has to do with love of place. I love the Fill, and all the birds in it. I love seeing something new here that I never saw before. Doing so expands my understanding. It strengthens my connection to nature and gives me a small window into the divine.

More than anything, it gives me a way to reconcile my two worlds. The Fill was made by humans when we built the Ship Canal to connect Lake Washington to Puget Sound. We lowered the lake and brought forth the land. But nature remade what we did. It seeded the Fill with plants, created ponds as the peat under the Fill compressed, enticed birds here, provided habitat for coyotes and river otters.

Together, nature and humans created a paradise.

Unlike ancient Eden, real paradises on Earth are not always peaceful, but they are always beautiful, at least to me. Often my little piece of paradise makes me smile, as I did when I saw the minuscule battles of the Green-winged Teals. Maybe some day, I think, we humans can learn to keep our battles as small.

I believe we can. I believe we will. The Fill, for me, is the embodiment of such hopes. And I don't need technological gadgets or even civilization to appreciate that.

6. Neither Fish nor Fowl

The little flock of seven Cackling Geese was paddling around in the lake near Canoe Island again today. They've been here all winter, but they won't stay much longer. They are tundra breeders, and soon they will heed the call of the Far North. When the wind blows in from the south one day, they will lift their heads and study the sky briefly, and then they will take off. Perhaps they will circle the Fill once or twice, as I have seen them do many times in the past few weeks. But instead of studying the fields to select just the right one for succulent grass, they will give their distinctive yipping call, and then they'll be gone, heading for a place I have never been, never seen, except in my imagination.

Cackling Geese are a recently named species. Formerly, they were considered to be a subspecies of our familiar Canada Geese, just a lot smaller. The smallest Cacklers are scarcely larger than Mallards and come equipped with dinky beaks. *Really* dinky beaks. But a few years ago, the American Ornithological Union (AOU), the folks who decree which birds shall merit species designations and which shall not, decided the Cacklers were different enough from Canadas to deserve their own species name. Furthermore, no one had observed the tiny Cacklers interbreeding with the ginormous Canadas, so there you go.

It was easy today to see why the AOU had come to this decision. When the Cacklers flew from the lake to Hunn Meadow East and began foraging beside two Canada Geese, the differences were dramatic. As I was studying both species, a jogger happened by. "Gosh,"

Cackling Goose © Doug Parrott

she said, "I didn't realize the geese were having babies so early. Just look at those cute little guys."

"Oh, those aren't baby Canada Geese," I replied. "They're a completely different species of goose. They're Cacklers."

There was a long, silent pause. Then, "Don't all geese cackle?" the jogger asked.

Without thinking, I said, "Oh my goodness, no. These geese yip. They're like terriers."

We stared at each other as we both processed how little sense I had just made. I grinned foolishly. The jogger back-pedaled a few feet, carefully keeping me in view. When she judged she had put enough distance between us, she turned and ran off.

I looked around for the nearest fence. Clearly, I needed to sit on it for a while, swing my feet aimlessly à la John Cleese in *Monty Python's Flying Circus,* and chant, "Doh-de-doh-de-doh." For once again, birding had made me look like the village idiot.

I experience this a lot, as many birders do. It seems to come with the territory. There was the time, for example, when I attended a family picnic at Seward Park. It was a fine summer day, and the picnic areas were packed with people. I had brought along my binoculars, hoping to spot the flock of Scarlet-fronted Parakeets that have made the park their home for the past several years. The parrots are nonmigratory natives of South America, so no one is sure how they got to Seattle. The theory is, some pet owner got fed up with the birds' constant noise and flung them out into a habitat they have found very appealing. They apparently started to breed, and now there is a whole flock that frequents the park.

I was sitting at a picnic table, eating my hot dog, when I heard the flock arrive in a nearby fir tree. Throwing my unfinished wiener onto my plate, I shot over to the tree, where I stood looking up into the boughs. I couldn't see a single parrot, so I circled around to another vantage point. Still no parrots. Naturally, I began to circle faster and faster, trying to get a good look. I also started to talk to myself. "Show yourselves, you stupid parrots."

Looking back on it, I confess it would have been hard to tell whether I most resembled one of the three Weird Sisters orbiting my magical cauldron, or a circus clown motoring around the center ring on my too-small motorcycle. Just as I was beginning my fourth circuit, I felt someone tug at my sleeve. It was my niece. "Come along, Aunt Connie," she said, "let's go back to the table and finish our hot dog."

"But the parrots," I protested, gesticulating wildly parrot-ward.

"Sit down," my niece hissed more commandingly in my ear. "Everyone is staring."

I looked around. Sure enough, everyone in the picnic area had stopped eating—some with their potato salad halfway to their mouths—and they were all looking at me. Meanwhile, the parrots had somehow disappeared as though they had never been. I slunk back to my hot dog and sat down. People resumed eating, but I noticed they kept looking at me sideways, I suppose to make sure I wouldn't pop off again.

Richard Feynman, the physics Nobel laureate, talked about how different he always felt from his fellow human beings. Then he fell in love with the most popular girl in town, Arlene. Much to his amazement, she fell in love with him, too, and they got married. It turned out they both felt different from other people, and they both thought this was a big plus. Their mantra became: What do *you* care what other people think?

Unfortunately, Arlene contracted terminal tuberculosis, and she gradually began to sink. At last, confined to her hospital room, she spent her days playing games with a world she was soon bound to exit. One day, when Feynman visited, she presented him with a small outdoor grill. She wanted him to cook steaks for her. Feynman objected, saying it wasn't safe to have a fire in her hospital room.

"All you have to do is take it out on the lawn. Then you can cook steaks every Friday," she said.

Feynman was horrified. The hospital was on Route 66, the main drag through town. "With all the cars and trucks going by, all the

Western Scrub-Jay © Kathrine Lloyd

people on the sidewalk walking back and forth, I can't just go out there and start cookin' steaks on the lawn!"

"What do *you* care what other people think?" Arlene asked. Then she hauled out a chef's hat and gloves and a big apron with writing on it: Bar-B-Q King. "We'll compromise," she said. "You don't have to wear the hat and the gloves."

So Feynman cooked steaks on Route 66 every weekend. He had to prove to his wife that he didn't care what other people thought.

Yet we do care. I guess it's because we are social animals. When your survival depends on getting along in a group, you have to pay attention to what other people do and say. You have to keep them at least marginally pleased with you so the group doesn't expel you into the netherworld of solitude and isolation where, without the help of others, you cannot survive for long. It is bred into our genes to care what other people think.

But Feynman and his wife were right, too. We are not *just* social creatures. We are also individuals, and as such, we have the gift of creating our own life as we see fit. To do that successfully, we must get over the fear of being different. I remember talking to my 97-year-old aunt about this just before she died. Aunt Marie had always loved people, but she was so shy, she never fit in. At parties or other gatherings, she would attach herself to a lively group of people and listen avidly to all they had to say, but she could never bring herself to add anything to the conversation. So quiet was she that oftentimes people didn't even realize she was there.

"Then when I was 85, I quit being shy," she said. "I realized it didn't matter, at my age, what anyone else thought of me. I could say anything and do anything, and people would just look at me, nod their heads, and whisper, 'Well, she's 85, you know.'

"Don't wait until you're 85 to realize it doesn't really matter what other people think of you," she concluded. "What matters most is what *you* think of you."

A few weeks later, I was somnambulating at a meeting of the Friends of Yesler Swamp. Not that the meeting or the speakers were boring, mind you. On the contrary, the speakers were substantial people who knew what they were talking about, and they were talking about an issue I am very interested in: the future of Yesler Swamp, the easternmost part of the Fill. But the afternoon was warm and sunny—one of the last remnants of the summer we should have had back in June or July but never did. The windows of the conference room were open, the air was balmy, and the voices started to fall into a rhythm akin to white noise. My eyes glassed over, and I found my mind drifting into a dream state, a kind of waking sleep similar to what fish, who have no eyelids and thus always look glassy-eyed, must experience. The last time I can remember falling into this state was in high school calculus class, a class I had to drop eventually due to complete lack of mathematical brain cells. My last thought, as I drifted off, was, "I hope no one calls on me."

Suddenly, a cobalt blue shape streaked by the window, calling its creaky gate-hinge call. "That's a scrub-jay," I yelled, leaping up and waving my arms like Ray Bolger fresh off the scarecrow pole.

Western Scrub-Jays are a kind of blue jay originally from California. Since the 1970s, they have been expanding their range northward. I saw my first one at the Fill two years ago, a bird that showed up in the company of our resident Steller's Jays, hung around for a couple of days, and then disappeared. The bird I saw at my meeting was only the second one I'd ever seen here. I tell you this so you will realize I was *justifiably* thrilled when it flew across the CUH yard like a glorious blue comet. Thrilled, not nuts.

Everyone else began to look wildly around for the source of my excitement. One woman, as I recall, even looked under the chairs at the floor—I guess all she heard me say clearly was the word "scrub." Of course, the bird itself had long ago vanished.

"IT'S ALL RIGHT," trumpeted a professor on the committee. "It's all right," he repeated more quietly. "She's a birder."

Everyone sat down again. The meeting resumed. I tried to look normal. A few minutes later, when a Northern Flicker flew in and attached itself to a wooden beam only a few feet away from the window, I didn't say a word. I had had enough attention for one day.

7. Dancing with Two Stars

When I turned a tomboyish twelve, my mother decided it was time to socially refine me. So she signed me up for ballroom dancing classes. A friend of hers, in cahoots, signed up her twelve-year-old son. The results, for a girl more interested in sports than in deportment, were all too predictable. My cha-cha was more of a chug-chug. My box step never broke out of the box. And since we girls were all taller than the boys, my swing dance looked more like the limbo whenever my partner tried in vain to twirl me under his upraised arm. As the popular limbo lyric asked, "How low can you go?"

I couldn't wait for the class to end, after which I vowed never to set foot in a ballroom again.

My vow broke, though, on a Friday in winter when I found myself attending a grand ball at the Fill. Oh, not in any of the CUH's buildings. This one was staged in nature itself, and its stars were two Belted Kingfishers. I was privileged to have a front-row seat on my camp stool. The show began, as such affairs often do, with the pair making a dramatic entrance. The female came first, swooping in from the marina and chattering her castanets. The male followed, trailing his wings like a cape. Ah, I thought, the passionate, Spanish-inspired paso doble. The two circled each other, now almost touching, now flying apart. Then the male hovered in place while his partner danced all around him in a wild clatter of skirts. So fiery was she that one of her feathers flew off and blew away on the wind.

Then the mood changed; the dance became a languid waltz, with the pair drifting over the bay and dancing back as one, swirling around each other in endless spirals of beauty. I found myself nodding in time to the unheard music. A Strauss air, without a doubt. The minutes passed, and still the pair danced, on and on without pause. I watched for more than an hour, almost hypnotized by the slow rhythm.

But then the mood changed yet again, as the two flew apart into different corners of the ballroom. I sat up on my camp stool. Something dramatic was about to happen. It began with the pair flying furiously toward each other, crossing in midair, turning back, crossing again, then circling to draw vast O's and X's in the sky. Finally, they joined for the most spectacular of all dance runs: the grand passage of the quickstep. In a diagonal flown across the entire Fill, the two danced intertwined, wing beat matching wing beat, swoop following swoop, the moves too quick for the eye to follow. I thought my heart would stop.

Just as they were starting their second grand pass, another male appeared and tried to cut in. The first male objected. A fight ensued. The female, no shy flower, egged on her chevalier from the sidelines. But as the fight continued, she seemed to realize she had lost their focus. She tilted her head, puzzled. "Wha'?" she seemed to ask herself, "I, no longer the center of attention? This cannot be." With a final (probably unprintable) remark, she flounced off the stage and went home.

Dance floor dudgeon. How well I understood.

Although I have never before witnessed the courtship flight of the kingfisher, I was not surprised to see it so early in the year. Winter is the season when many birds establish or strengthen the pair bond that will result in new life in spring. Male Mallards, for example, come out of their cryptic camouflage feathers of brown by December and parade themselves in the gemstone greens, purples, and whites that make these ducks such a standout to the girls.

Lately, the little male Eurasian Teal (the Siberian form of our American Green-winged Teal) has been busy shedding his drab plumage for a brighter set of green and chestnut on his head, gray Glen checks on his flanks, and a flourish of tan on his tail. This is his second season with us. Eurasian Teals usually spend the winter in Southeast Asia, not North America, but two years ago, this little guy goofed when he headed south on his first migration and ended up here. He must have liked it, because he came back in November, looking scruffy after a summer in the Arctic.

Now that the mating season is beginning, he is trying as hard as he can to get with the program. Week by week, I have watched him gradually become more and more attractive. Yesterday, he must have figured he was good to go, because he swam over to a female and began ratcheting his head up and down, the teal version of "hey baby, hey baby, hey baby."

So far, the females are ignoring him. It's hard for a guy to find the right girl. Or, as my husband likes to say, for a girl to get a guy to think he's found the right girl. That's true whether you're a duck or a person. All three of our twenty-something children, for example, are at that stage of life now. My daughter calls it "finding the One."

She and her friends like to ask my advice about the One. I guess they figure that since John and I have been married for 31 years, we must know a little something. It's highly gratifying to me that these young people want my opinion. They are, after all, not so distant from the teenage years, when they thought I had the IQ of a daffodil, and not a very bright one at that.

I'm still getting used to this new phase. The other day, when one of our daughter's friends learned the lengthiness of love that John and I have shared, she asked, "You mean to tell me you've been together more than *30 years?* That's awesome."

She said this with the same wide-eyed expression I imagine Moses must have worn when the Burning Bush tried to tell him a thing or two. Quickly, I moved to take advantage of this rare, teachable moment.

"In the beginning," I intoned, "you must find the One who brings out the best in you, who will help you achieve your dreams, and whom you can help in the same way. Then you must identify the values you hold most dear, and establish the same values as a couple. After that, you can sweat the small stuff that doesn't really matter because you've already handled the big stuff. Take the other night, for example. John and I..."

My daughter's friend began to check the time on her iPhone. "I'd love to hear your story," she began, "but I have to..."

"The other night," I repeated relentlessly, as she sighed and sank back into her chair, "John and I were watching Celtic Thunder on PBS. That's the group of five singers, or maybe it's six now—I can't keep track. Anyway, they're the guys from Ireland who sing a mixture of folk songs and pop. One of them began to sing a Scottish song, and out comes a bagpipe player wearing a kilt. 'That's not Celtic,' said John. 'That's Scottish.'

"'Scottish is Celtic,' I replied."

Whereupon, as I explained to my now nearly comatose audience, John and I got into a meaningless quarrel about whether the Scots are Celts. After a brisk exchange in which facts were mere figments of imagination to be tossed around, John turned to Google. Google, I will point out, like so many other human inventions of consequence, is both a blessing and a curse. A blessing when it proves I am right, a curse when it says I am not. In this case, Google gave me its blessing, to John's disgust.

"The point is," I said, trying to revive my daughter's friend, who had definitely nodded off by this time, "our argument really was meaningless. It was a bit of fluff we were batting back and forth for fun because we don't have to argue about the important things anymore. We just have to live them."

With that, I released my captive audience, who fled gratefully into the night. When I told John (a.k.a. the Great Homily-Giver) about this experience, he said, "The mistake you made was you monologued. That's why your audience went to sleep. You need to be able to put your homilies on a bumper sticker."

"Like what?" I asked.

John thought for a second. "In the dance of life, what matters is not where you start from, but where you come together."

Not bad, eh? I think I'll keep him.

Male Belted Kingfisher © Thomas Sanders

8. This Song Is about You

Male Buffleheads are the Beau Brummells of duckdom. Brummell, you may recall, was the maven of male fashion for the haut ton of Regency England. He believed in elegant simplicity and so invented the black tie and tails that men still wear to posh events today. Like Brummell, Buffleheads believe in being starkly dramatic in their dress: black backs, white breasts and flanks, a wedge of white on their black heads. But unlike the Beau, Buffleheads can't quite resist the urge to accessorize. In breeding season, they sport red feet so bright they would turn Dorothy green with envy. When a male Bufflehead lowers his landing gear in bright sunlight, he is a living jewel box of glory: rubies, opal, and jet. He acquires even more jewel tones when the light catches his iridescent black feathers and transforms them into emerald and amethyst.

Meanwhile, his drab mate floats discreetly nearby, an understated sketch of charcoal and smudgy white.

Looks can deceive, however, for it is the female who is the star of the Bufflehead show. Although female Buffleheads are our smallest diving duck, they are packed from head to webbed toe with aggression. They nest in old woodpecker holes in the boreal forests of Alaska, Canada, and the northeast corner of our own state, where they fight all comers who might try to claim a piece of their territory. Ideally, the female Bufflehead's tree hole of choice is near a pond or lake, where the chicks can feed after they hatch. Good holes are hard to find. A female who comes across one will return to it year after year, defending it fiercely against interlopers.

As winter gives way to spring down here in the balmy south of their range, the female Buffleheads start to ramp up their aggression. I've seen females fly across the entire length of Yesler Cove to attack each other over the possession of a mate. Buffleheads often keep the same mates from one year to the next, but that doesn't mean a rival female will refrain from trying to steal a guy who is already spoken for. Meanwhile, as the females duke it out, the male in dispute puffs out his little chest and rears halfway up out of the water. Clearly, he believes he is well worth fighting over. "Ain't I fine?" you can almost hear him ask. And I find myself quietly humming the Carly Simon song, "You're So Vain."

In another few weeks, when the nights grow short and the days get long, the Buffleheads will leave for the north, taking a piece of my heart with them. I have never been to the forests where the Buffleheads breed, never seen a smudgy duck-head improbably peeking out from a tree hole, never watched the chicks teeter on the edge of the hole before plummeting to the ground, unhurt.

In a certain sense, I don't have to go up north bodily because I can see all this in my mind's eye, thanks to researchers and videographers who have gone to the trouble of hiking the trackless wilderness favored by these ducks. Others endured the bite of the black fly, the scratch of the scrub brush, the rock digging into the back at night, all so that Motel 6 birders like me can see these wonders of nature through their eyes and cameras, without leaving the comforts of our warm television sets.

The BBC's recent series *Planet Earth* is a good example of the work these researchers do. One episode, entitled "Seasonal Forests," shows a female Mandarin Duck, the Siberian relative of our own Wood Duck, nesting in a tree hole somewhere in Russia. The female has hatched a brood of nine ducklings, and she needs to persuade her babies to jump out of their tree so they can walk to a pond almost a mile away to eat. Like most other ducks, Mandarins don't bring food to their hatchlings, so the babies have no choice but to leave the nest and follow their mom to the nearest food source. As we watch, the female calls to her babies from the forest floor, and two by two,

Female Bufflehead © Tim Kuhn

the babies plunge dozens of feet to the ground, bounce once or twice on the spongy leaf litter, and stand up, none the worse.

We aren't told how the BBC photographers found this tree in the middle of the forest, nor how many days they waited for the blessed event to happen. We don't even know how the photographers managed to follow the duck family—at duck level!—through the forest to the pond.

We *are* told, however, about a similar effort in New Guinea, where Paul Stewart, the BBC photographer, sat in a bird blind for nearly five weeks, waiting for a female Six-plumed Bird-of-Paradise to show up at a jungle bower meticulously prepared and maintained by the male. The producers wanted to show us the male's display dance. Unfortunately, although the male worked very hard to keep his bower attractively tidy, no female appeared. Day after weary day, the bird-of-paradise puttered, picking up leaves and taking them out to the trash. He polished his perch and groomed himself several times a day. Meanwhile, Stewart sat in his dark, hot blind for up to nine hours at a stretch, peering through a peephole, unable to stop humming Marty Robbins's cloying song "Sweet Bird of Paradise." Over and over. Until he thought he would go mad.

Finally, a female arrived, the male put on his little dance, and the unimpressed female flew off. The entire encounter lasted seven seconds. End of show.

As amazing as it is that any human being would try so hard and suffer so much for such a small reward, I wish these nutty researchers would work even harder. There is much that still needs to be explored about the hidden lives of birds. What do birds do at night? Do they stay awake, watching for predators, or do they sleep soundly? Where do they go? Considering the number of birds we see at the Fill all day long, why don't the surrounding trees sport roosting birds by the dozen at dusk, hanging on branches like Christmas ornaments? When birds disappear into the dense cattails or thick grass, what are they up to? Do they stride between the plant stems, or hunker down, hopping to the next place when they want to move? When the diving birds upend their tails and sink underwater, what happens to them? Is it hard for them to find prey, or are the fish, crustaceans, and plants abundant for the taking?

The reason I think it's so important for an army of intrepid researchers to get cracking for the rest of us is because of a discovery made by the garbologist William Rathje. Rathje was an archaeologist at the University of Arizona. Back in the 1970s, he was trying to figure out how to train student archaeologists in the art of the dig. He wanted to give them practical experience about how to correlate physical remains with human behavior. He realized that if his students could sort through garbage from selected homes, they could make all kinds of connections about how people live. Thus, the Garbage Project was born. Eventually, Rathje and his students invented a whole new science: garbology, the study of the things we humans discard, and the stories we tell ourselves about them.

One of the most common stories we tell ourselves is: Out of sight, out of mind. Few of us pay any attention to our garbage after we throw it in the can or haul it out to the street on pickup day. Where does it go? What happens to it after it arrives at its destination? How much of it is there? Who knows?

Rathje and his students discovered we live in profound ignorance about our trash. We rely, instead, on myths. According to Rathje's book *Rubbish!*, when the Garbage Project asked National Audubon Society members which items took up the most volume in landfills, they estimated that polystyrene foam occupied from 20 to 40 percent of the volume; disposable diapers between 25 and 45 percent; and fast-food packaging between 20 and 30 percent. The Garbage Project's actual figures are: 1 percent for polystyrene; 1.4 percent for disposable diapers; and 0.33 percent for fast-food waste.

Other myths abound: that trash in sanitary landfills decomposes over time (it doesn't); that biodegradable products in a landfill are better than non-biodegradable ones (they aren't; both just sit there inertly); that people generate more waste now than in the past (they don't, when you consider no one discards coal ash anymore, or manure, or dead horses, or hundreds of pounds of spoiled food due to lack of refrigeration).

Mythologies of this epic size have a big impact on public policy decisions. Which brings me back to the birds. If we know so little—and think so little—about what birds do when we aren't watching them, how can we make good decisions about habitat management?

In the coming decades, I believe habitat management will occupy an even greater role in environmentalism than it does today. The United Nations Population Division, which makes biennial projections of world population, just released its latest findings. It estimates that by 2050, the number of humans on the planet will be more than 9 billion. That is up from 6.8 billion today. The good news is, more people will live in cities, which helps preserve wild lands. Unfortunately, the strain on resources may make that fact irrelevant, as demand for fresh water, raw minerals, energy, food, and building materials is growing even faster than population. That's because people in developing countries want to achieve a higher standard of living. These demands will inevitably affect the preservation of habitat for wild animals, even more than they do today.

Globalization will also continue to increase. That means there will be ever more contacts among peoples of the world. This could be a great thing for world peace, but it could also mean the introduction of more invasive species into habitats that are ill equipped to control them. Global climate change will affect the biota as well, in effect moving the tropics into temperate zones, the temperate zones into tundra, and the tundra into oblivion.

Everything I see at the Fill tells me the only solution to these problems that preserves species diversity and integrity is moderation. If we humans can moderate our impact on the planet, if we can slow or stop our population growth, mitigate its ill effects by creating sustainable lifestyles, and—above all—respect the needs of the natural world, then a remarkable number of species seem able to fit themselves around human activities. The species are still affected, but many can hang on and adapt. They can survive.

Buffleheads are a good example. When they come back to us in the late fall, they will find a lake loaded with boats. The boats are filled with people who aren't always careful about keeping the lake clean. Day and night, the Buffleheads will be bombarded by the constant noise of city life. There is never a moment that is completely quiet. Neither will Buffleheads ever spend a night in total darkness here as they would up north, because the city lights are never turned off. The lake provides small fish for them to eat, but many of the fish living in Lake Washington now are non-natives. Yet despite all these human impacts, the Buffleheads seem, to my nonbirdly eye, to be happy here. So happy, in fact, that when spring rolls around again in its never-ending cycle, there are always a few Buffleheads who seem reluctant to leave. They put off going north, where their hormones tell them they're supposed to be. Some of them procrastinate so long, they're still here when their cousins arrive again in November. "Where did the time go?" they seem to ask, looking faintly surprised at the returning newcomers.

The Buffleheads do well here thanks in large part to people who cleaned up the pollution that was choking the life out of the lake and who saw to it that the Fill became—and still is—a natural area. Because of their efforts, Buffleheads have places to go where it's safe for them to tuck their bills into their back feathers and go to sleep.

Because we respect the Buffleheads' needs, we will be able to enjoy all their little dramas for years to come. As I watch the females jousting this season, and the males showing off, I feel a small sense of pride that we have given these birds a decent winter home. It is a success story I hope we can extend all over the planet.

Queen Anne's Lace © Jean Colley

Part II
Spring

9. This Means War

I always think of February in Seattle as a spring month. It is the time when the crocuses come up, the pussy willows bud, and the daffodil spears rise up out of the still-chilled ground. However, much as I anticipate the coming of spring, even I must admit that February can also carry a hefty winter punch. This is especially true in a La Niña year, when a pool of cold water forms in the Pacific and chills the West Coast for months. La Niñas can vary in strength. The one we're experiencing this year has been especially strong, delaying spring and putting a heavy burden of dim days and low temperatures on all us Seattleites, avian and human alike.

So it was as I walked along Surber Drive yesterday in the early morning. Surber Drive marks the eastern border of the Fill and parallels Yesler Swamp for a block or two. The sun was up, but the swamp was still dark, shadowed by a ridge to the east and the houses lining the far side of the street. Only the tips of the trees were bathed in light, and none of the birds were stirring. The rusty-colored stream that pools along the edge of the swamp was frozen solid—no telling what its freezing point was, considering all the weirdly colored chemicals that wash down from the streets and lawns of the neighborhood and pollute the water. Judging from the lack of feeling in my toes, though, the temperature must have been 50 below, despite the Weather Channel's assurances that it was really a toasty 31 degrees.

I set down my camp stool just as the sun topped the ridge. My multiple layers of shirts, vests, and jacket bunched up around my throat, threatening to choke me. I sighed. I have become so tired of bundling up like the Michelin Man. How I yearn for warm days to come. The yearning was so great on this arctic day, I leaned forward on my stool. I could almost feel my soul trying to jump out of my mouth and head south. "Maybe that's what's really choking me," I thought. Then, "Must get a grip."

As I struggled to control my whines, a flurry of Black-capped Chickadees swirled over to the tree above my head. Chickadees flock together for protection during the winter months, but these chickadees were far from any attempt at togetherness. On the contrary, they were arguing over territory. The fight escalated into a smackdown, with six chickadees going at each other all at once. The fight became so intense they lost sight of the dangers a human might pose. The next thing I knew, the fight was churning around my head, and I was ducking and weaving as fast as the chickadees. One bird almost biffed me in the eye. "Hey," I said.

The fight stopped. Each chickadee retired to his own branch and fluffed his feathers. "Behave yourselves," I started to admonish, but a hidden bell must have rung, and they were at it again. Luckily, the ball of fighting chickadees rolled off over the treetops, and I was alone. Their hormones had carried them away.

Ah, spring—when a young bird's fancy turns to showing rivals a thing or two. I packed up my camp stool and headed for the Wedding Rock. I wanted to see if the Anna's Hummingbird who has been on guard there all winter long was still okay. The CUH folks put out a feeder of sugar water year-round for the hummers, but even so, it's a wonder such tiny birds can survive the cold. It is said that when the winter sun goes down and the temperatures fall, Anna's Hummingbirds go into hibernation for the night. The coming dawn is supposed to revive them each day, but what happens when the dawn brings no warmth? Larger birds tuck their bills into their back feathers to stay warm, but hummingbirds have so much bill area to heat, relative to their bodies, how do they do it?

Pondering this question, I looked around the tops of the bushes for my guy. I found him facing the sun. He paid no attention to me.

Male Anna's Hummingbird © Kathrine Lloyd

Instead, he was gearing up for battle. Anna's do this by fluffing out their magenta gorgets and shining them at their rivals.

The word *gorget* comes from the medieval term for armor that covered the throat. An Anna's gorget, however, covers a lot more than just the throat. It is the whole-head kind, stretching from the top of the bird's head down the neck and over the throat all the way to the shoulders (if hummingbirds had shoulders). When their iridescent feathers catch the light full-on, the color is so intense it hurts your eyes. No painter can duplicate it; no photographer can capture it; no words can describe it. If you really want to understand an Anna's impact, you must find one in spring and position yourself with your back to the sun. Bring along some sunglasses, if you have weak eyes.

The Battle of the Gorgets is not the end-all of a hummingbird duel. It's just the opening sally. The next round consists of the male lifting himself skyward as though he were riding an invisible ferris wheel straight to heaven. When he gets up high enough, he pauses and then rockets toward the earth. Just before impact, he hauls up his nose and spreads out his tail. The tail feathers utter a shriek so loud you can hear it 50 meters away. Lesser males are supposed to flee in utter terror. Meanwhile, the female is—theoretically, at least—duly impressed.

If this fails to rout the rival, the Anna's tries direct action, shooting like a bullet toward the other male. I don't recommend getting in the middle of one of these duels. I did once, without even knowing a fight was in progress. My situational awareness must have been fast asleep at the switch. We both came to when a male shot past, right under the brim of my hat. I think if I had been wearing hoop earrings, I would have lassoed him. "Oi!" I shouted, but the culprit was long gone.

Although birds can get very caught up in their battles for territory, food, and females, most of the time they have an "off" switch that prevents them from killing each other when they fight. One male usually senses that he is losing, so he turns tail and flies away. The other male always lets him go, as soon as the rival passes an invisible territorial boundary. This allows an opponent to live to fight another day, but it's not altruism or wisdom that makes the winner behave in this fashion. He's probably too scared to venture far in the chase because as soon as he crosses his own boundary, he enters the territory of another male as aggressive as he is about defending the home front.

Ornithologists say there is another reason bird fights are relatively benign. Most fights, they say, are not really fights at all, in the way we humans define a fight. Many times, all a male has to do to chase away a rival is show off his breeding plumage. If his feathers are bright enough, and if his confidence in flashing them is great enough, the other males simply fold their own feathers and leave.

Avoiding physical contact makes a lot of sense. Fighting is very risky. Most birds' bones are fragile, filled with air sacs to lighten them for flight. It's easy for a bird to break a bone. If that happens to a wing bone, making flight impossible, the bird is doomed.

Back in the days of the Cold War, the Russians and Americans understood this. As soon as the Soviet Union acquired nuclear technology and built A-bombs and then H-bombs, both sides realized the consequences of direct battle were too dire to contemplate. So instead, we shined our arsenals at each other, as we still do. Every May 1, for example, the Soviets parade their enormous missiles through Red Square, showing off their might. We, on the other hand, make sure the Russians always know how many kilotons are aimed right at them, and how inaccessible our missile platforms are.

Such posturing has facilitated the signing of treaties among the nuclear powers and has aided our mutual efforts to keep weapons of mass destruction out of the hands of other countries. But it has not prevented smaller, conventional wars. Since the Cold War ended in 1991, humans have engaged in scores of wars or other military actions that resulted in the deaths of thousands of people. By some measures, no day in the past 30 years has gone by without some military killing somewhere on the planet.

By contrast, I have never witnessed even one war to the death at the Fill. That's not to say I see no death here. Prey die routinely at the

Male Red-winged Blackbird displaying © Kathrine Lloyd

Fill, as Bald Eagles kill coots and ducks; grebes and cormorants kill fish; and swallows and warblers kill insects. Even as babies, birds can kill. Take baby Brown-headed Cowbirds, for example, whose parasitic parents sneak into the nests of other birds to lay eggs that the hosts will raise. The cowbird babies hatch before the hosts' real babies do, enabling the cowbirds to crush the other eggs so they can monopolize their foster parents' attention and care.

Death, in fact, is all around us in nature, but death is not war. Rather, it is part of the circle of life. As King Mufasa saccharinely explained to his son Simba in Disney's *The Lion King,* "Everything you see exists together in a delicate balance. As king, you need to understand that balance and respect all the creatures, from the crawling ant to the leaping antelope."

Young Simba is confused. "But Dad, don't we eat the antelope?"

"Yes, Simba, but let me explain. When we die, our bodies become the grass, and the antelope eat the grass. And so we are all connected in the great Circle of Life."

War, by contrast, exists outside the circle—for animals, that is, but not for us. War is systematic, communal. It is fueled by hate, greed, and fear. It is, many would argue, part of human nature.

Mark Twain, in his *Letters from the Earth,* explained human nature thusly. He wrote that God decided to create a great experiment in morals and character. He began by creating all the animals and endowing each one with a certain nature. Satan, observing the animals' behavior, is surprised when he sees some animals murdering others. "This large beast is killing weaker animals, Divine One," he says.

"The tiger—yes," God says. "The law of his nature is ferocity. The law of his nature is the Law of God. He cannot disobey it."

"Then," says Satan, trying to get clear on all this, "in obeying it he commits no offense, Divine One?"

"No, he is blameless."

"This other creature, here, is timid, Divine One, and suffers death without resisting."

"The rabbit—yes. He is without courage. It is the law of his nature—the Law of God. He must obey it."

"Then he cannot honorably be required to go counter to the law of his nature and resist, Divine One?"

"No. No creature can be honorably required to go counter to the law of his nature—the Law of God."

God goes on to show Satan his greatest creation: Man. He tells Satan he has endowed Man with all the various moral qualities he has singly given to each of the animals. It's a long list: courage, cowardice, ferocity, gentleness, fairness, justice, cunning, treachery, magnanimity, cruelty, malice, malignity, lust, mercy, pity, purity, selfishness, sweetness, honor, love, hate, baseness, nobility, loyalty, falsity, veracity, untruthfulness.

Twain, with characteristic satire, goes on to claim that no person can be blamed for any wrongdoing, nor anyone praised for good, because each of us is merely following our immutable nature, as given by God.

We more modern types know, however, that people are quite mutable. Science has shown us that our neurons can keep growing, and our synapses can keep making new connections throughout life. No matter what traits we are born with, we can grow new neurons, make new connections, and acquire different traits, changing ourselves in ways that we ourselves can direct.

The instincts that drive most of animal behavior are present in us, too, of course, but our instincts are such a mishmash of competing traits, we cannot follow just one and claim it is "human nature." For what, exactly, is human nature?

Twain said each of us has within us both good and evil. War is part of our nature, but so is peace. Hate is part of us, but so is love. Since we are capable of living both in the dark and in the light, we have the power—more than that, the obligation—to choose.

The chickadees fight because their preprogrammed DNA tells their glands to make hormones that raise the level of aggression. Our DNA does the same, but unlike a chickadee, we don't have to listen solely to it. Stupid DNA.

Who we are is largely up to us. How we act is also largely up to us. *That* is our true nature.

10. Symphony in D Flat for Cormorants

Double-crested Cormorants are not the Grace Kellys of the avian world. Their proportions are all wrong, for one thing. Their necks are too long, and their tails are too short. When they fly, they install a kink in their necks to even up the proportions, but it is a temporary fix, and not a pretty one.

Neither are their voices pretty. When they call, I don't hear the evocative tones of the wild and lonely gulls, or the comforting quacks of the ducks. Rather, I hear the cranky noise of discordance. Cormorants sound like my old car used to when I was learning how to drive a stick shift. I habitually ground the gears, making my husband wince and my dental fillings whine.

Cormorants have other issues as well. You might say Double-crested Cormorants are a walking, talking, flying contradiction in terms. They have webbed feet like ducks, but they perch in trees like robins. They are water birds, but their feathers are not waterproof. After they dive for fish, they have to hang their wings out to dry. In early spring, you can often see them perched on the log boom in the lake, with their laundry on the line, as it were: arms outstretched, wing feathers gently waving in the dank, humid air of a cold Seattle April. I've hung laundry out myself then, and I can tell you, neither clothes nor feathers are going to get dry very fast in this climate. You'd think a hundred million years or so of evolution would have created a water bird better suited to the water, but no.

Double-crested Cormorant drying its wings © Doug Parrott

As for their romantically dubbed "double crests," we don't see them much here at the Fill. The birds tend to leave for their breeding grounds before they are totally decked out to appeal to the opposite sex. Even if we did see the crests, I'm not sure they would add anything to the birds' gravitas. Probably the opposite, for the crests are not exactly crests at all. They are white or black tufts that sprout outlandishly near the birds' eyes, kind of like a grandpa whose eyebrows have been watered with too much Rogaine.

And yet. Grace Kelly might very well have swooned with envy at the beauty of these birds, whose eyes are the color of jade and whose faintly iridescent black feathers are edged with even deeper black. No one in the bird kingdom wears the "little black dress" more elegantly than do cormorants. As awkward as they appear on land, they are grace itself in the water. They glide along the surface with their chins up, like runway models dressed in the latest Dior.

I love cormorants precisely because of their unlikely combination of goofiness and glam. When they gollop their food—and they always gulp their fish whole—they never look guilty at their lack of table manners. On the contrary, they toss their food around with gay abandon as they maneuver their catch to slide down the hatch head-first. Sometimes the fish is so large, I wonder how the cormorant is ever going to get it swallowed. I saw a bird out on the lake one morning who had caught a wide, pancake-shaped fish that wasn't designed to fit through a narrow, tube-shaped throat. The cormorant tried lining up the fish vertically, then horizontally, but it was the fish's diameter that presented a problem, not its alignment. Eventually, the cormorant shrugged its figurative shoulders, gave a mighty gulp, and somehow disappeared the fish. Then the cormorant spent the next several minutes plashing its wings in little claps, the way an appreciative dinner crowd might applaud the chef, the chef in this case being itself.

The cormorant, you see, is a bird that's comfortable in its own skin, at once fashionable and farouche. Most humans, by contrast, achieve this level of self-acceptance only after years of faux pas. For example, I still painfully recall the first ball I went to as a teenager.

I was in Missoula, Montana, at a summer speech camp. The camp ended with a big dance, to which the boy of my dreams miraculously invited me. Unfortunately, I hadn't brought proper clothes, so I had to borrow a dressy skirt from a friend. The skirt was too big, and my friend had to pin it. Naturally, no one had brought safety pins, so we snuck into a classroom and stole a straight pin from the teacher's desk. I thought all was well, not realizing the cow pie that the Three Fates had prepared for me to step in.

The Three Fates, you may recall, were the ancient Greeks' idea of destiny. The Greeks believed that seven days after a child was born, the Three Fates appeared at the child's door to spin the thread of the kid's future. The Greeks imagined the Three Fates as mean old hags, kind of reminiscent of three of my more fearsome aunts. No one was happy when they showed up, but you couldn't turn them away, either. You just had to hope they were in a good mood, didn't stay long, and exited without leaving too much rubble in their wake.

The Three Fates liked their little jokes and had prepared a doozy for me. The night of the dance was clear and warm, with a beautiful moon in the sky and a live band in the hall. My date and I danced the dances of the times, which consisted of us wiggling around on the dance floor with no particular steps or even rhythm. Eventually, we wandered out onto the veranda, where he cautiously reached his arm out to place around my waist. Then, "Ouch," he yelled, having impaled his hand on my straight pin.

The pin must have hit a small artery in his finger because he bled like the gusher of a Texas wildcat's oil strike. All my self-confidence in co-ed social events bled out just as copiously. What a ghastly affair. The poor boy probably suffered an even greater loss of self-confidence than I did. "Girls put pins in their skirts?" he must have thought. "How many do they put in? Do they put them in anywhere else? Omigod, omigod, omigod."

We humans walk a fine line between standing out and fitting in. We must work to stand out if we want to contribute our unique originality to the world. We are individuals, after all. But we must also try to fit in with others around us. We are social creatures, too.

Double-crested Cormorant © Tim Kuhn

To complicate matters, each of us is born with different degrees of talent in different areas. Some of us have great math aptitude, while others have better physical coordination. Some people are blessed with charm, others cursed with foot-in-mouth disease. None of these differences mean that much, however, because most of us are given the brainpower to overcome our own deficiencies. If we put our minds to it, we can learn almost anything.

How much can we learn, and how long will it take? My husband says there is no limit to how much we can learn. We are all geniuses, in his book. "Genius is 1 percent inspiration, 99 percent perspiration," he often says, quoting Thomas Edison.

As for the time it takes to learn something, John believes if we put in a thousand hours, we can get pretty good at any new skill. By "new skill," he means something roughly on the order of, say, Hamiltonian quantum mechanics. As proof of his thousand-hour theory, he offers the fact that that's about how long it took him to teach me how to properly drive a stick shift, a task at least as difficult as teaching me quantum physics.

While I might question John's estimate of the amount of time it takes for me to learn something new, I believe his overall theory is generally on the right track. For example, we all know that Wolfgang Amadeus Mozart wrote his first symphony at the age of eight. Everyone called him a child prodigy, but we forget he began studying music at age three. If Mozart worked only four hours a day on his music, he would have put in 5,800 hours by the time he was eight. So far from marveling at his child-prodigiousness, we might better ask what took him so long?

Okay, I admit that even if I studied for twice as long, I would not be able to write a symphony one-tenth as good as Mozart's childish effort. But if I had begun studying music at age three and worked at it for 30 hours a week for 58 years, now at the age of 61 I have no doubt I would be able to compose a symphony. Derivative, perhaps; pedestrian, possibly; respectable, surely.

The point is, we may be hindered or helped by the gifts we are born with, but we still have great freedom to accomplish whatever we set our minds to. Like the cormorant, if we lack waterproofed feathers, we should not let that minor fact keep us out of the water.

My daughter, for example, began studying dance when she was small. It was her passion. John and I used to go to her performances, and we were always enthralled. I can still close my eyes and picture her in "Wade in the Water," the Alvin Ailey-choreographed dance set to gospel music. My daughter's school has had a long tradition of performance art, and for graduation, the seniors always put on a show. My daughter chose to participate in the show, but not by dancing. Although she had never joined any of the school's numerous vocal ensembles, she decided that her graduation performance would be a song. I remember she wore a slim, full-length red gown. She walked to the front of the stage all alone. She told me later she felt petrified. She began singing too softly and slightly off-key, then rallied and finished the song beautifully. I asked her later what she had been trying to prove. "Nothing," she answered. "I just wanted to do something different."

So naturally, for years I tried to figure out what she had been trying to prove. Recently, I got it. After her high school graduation, she went on to college, where she proceeded to try all kinds of different things. She took up wind-surfing and soccer, although she had never done sports before. She joined a softball team. She went bungee jumping. For her 25th birthday, her boyfriend bought her a sky-dive. The company he chose provided videos of their customers' experiences. The video of my daughter shows her plunging out of the airplane with a huge smile on her face.

Ah. Now I understand. Like the cormorant who refused to wait for waterproofing before diving in, my daughter dives into life without waiting, either. She doesn't care if she's any good at what she tries. She just wants to try. She is comfortable in her own skin, but more important, she wants to experience how it feels to do something different, be someone different.

Fate has no hold on her. She shapes her own destiny, as—to a very large degree—we all can.

11. A Mother's Care

The two baby Killdeers who recently hatched at the Fill have already left their nest—a scrape in the gravel of the Dime Lot—and have begun foraging for themselves under the watchful eyes of their parents. You can see them running on their long legs amid the short grass that borders the gravel. They look like fuzzballs on stilts as they dart here and there searching for bugs and worms to eat.

Killdeers are precocial birds, meaning the babies are born with the ability to fend for themselves almost immediately after hatching. That's not to say they can dispense with their parents, however. On the contrary, baby Killdeers depend on their parents to show them the best spots to find food. The babies also rely on their parents to help ward off danger. Crows are always on the lookout for unwary younglings, and the Raccoons and Coyotes who hunt by night wouldn't say no to a tasty Killdeer either. It's a chancy world.

Parent Killdeers can't do much to fight off predators. They don't have the proper equipment. They lack sharp talons and don't carry any permits for concealed weapons. Outside of freezing into a statue and hoping their browns, blacks, whites, and beiges will conceal them from predators' eyes, Killdeer adults have only one mechanism to protect their young: They pretend to be injured themselves.

The parents at the Dime Lot are especially skilled at this. If they think I'm going to threaten their young, one of them will stick out a wing or a tail and drag it along brokenly on the ground, crying piteously to attract my attention. If I follow the "wounded" bird, it manages to stumble ahead just fast enough to keep from getting

Killdeer displaying "broken" wing © Kathrine Lloyd

caught. When it thinks it has drawn me far enough away, it leaps into the air, giving its characteristic "kill-EER, kill-EEER" laugh, and flounces away, leaving me empty-handed and feeling foolish. What a chump.

Unfortunately, this act is the only arrow in the Killdeers' quiver. I've often wondered how effective it is in fooling the Killdeers' foes. Crows, Raccoons, and Coyotes are among the brainiest of predators, and I suspect they subscribe to that old Chinese chestnut: "Fool me once, shame on you; fool me twice, shame on me." After the first time, I doubt these sly critters would follow a Killdeer again, no matter how realistically hurt it appears.

Perhaps that's why the Killdeer parents at the Dime Lot always seem to me to look so worried. As they stand guard over their babies, they repeatedly jerk their heads with uncontrollable tics, like Chief Inspector Dreyfus about to be clonged by the inept Inspector Clouseau for the 50th time in the Pink Panther spoofs. The Killdeers' brows are furrowed, their eyes dart all over, looking for danger. Meanwhile, the two babies are oblivious. They peck here, they peck there. They pay no attention to the adults' suggestions to stay close to cover. When a car drives into the lot, the two babies run out in front of it, barely escaping getting crushed by the wheels. The parents look ready to faint.

I clutch my chest in sympathy. I know just how they feel. My own kids are in their mid-20s, and they too believe they can get along just fine on their own. "We're adults now," they tell me in patronizing tones. But like the baby Killdeers, they sometimes rush in where angels fear to tread.

No wonder my brow is furrowed, my left eye twitches uncontrollably, and my hand frequently grabs my shirt buttons in a vain attempt to keep my heart installed in its chest. "Don't clutch," my kids say, as they take a corner too fast, or go off into the wilderness with one pair of shorts and a cheery wave.

Motherhood has been the greatest joy of my life, but I have to confess this phase of motherhood is not my favorite. There are too many times when the best thing I can do to help my kids is stay out of their way while they go ahead and take risks. I dislike the spectator role, sitting in the audience, watching a potential disaster-train speeding down the track. I feel so helpless.

When I first arrived at this stage of life, I thought perhaps I was overreacting because I was new to the Baby Birds Leaving the Nest Syndrome. I decided to consult some experts, so I went to my 97-year-old aunt's retirement home and buttonholed every old woman I could find. "Is this how it always is," I asked them, "or does it get better? Do you ever stop worrying to death about the risky things your kids get up to?"

The women looked at me like I had two heads, each dumber than a post. "Hello!" one said, pointing to her white hair. "Where do you think I got this? No, you never stop worrying."

Since then, I have struggled to learn how to live with my fears. I try not to foist my worries off on my kids. My worries are my own, and I must manage them myself. I cannot let my fears for their safety dictate to my kids the chances they take in life. How stifling that would be for them, and how unfair.

When the kids were small, I used to take them out birding with me from time to time. Once I drove them all the way to the Potholes in eastern Washington to look for desert birds. We hiked down to a pond out in the middle of a sagebrush wilderness, a true oasis in the desert, surrounded by cattails. As we approached the pond's edge, I heard a dry, rattling sound, like the wind rustling dead leaves. My oldest son, running far ahead, stopped short of a bush and cried, "It's a rattlesnake!"

Sure enough, coiled under the bush was a snake the size of an anaconda, poised to strike. Its eyes were fixed on my helpless child with a deadened, mummy-stare that showed no shred of kindness or pity or anything even vaguely emotional. I hate snakes, and this one was particularly nasty. However, I did not want to pass my fears on to my children, so instead of running around squawking like a chicken about to lose its head (which was my first reaction), I calmly looked at my watch and said, "Well, that is a nice snake, dear, but we have go. Right now."

I thought I had hidden my fear from my kids, but I was wrong. Not only did they realize I hate snakes, they also apparently made up their minds at that point not to expose me to things that might cause my hair to stand on end. To make sure I stayed pacified, they developed a calibration system that guided them as to when to reveal their escapades to me. Ordinary risks of day-to-day life would be disclosed in a week or two. More death-defying deeds might need to marinate for up to a year. The truly terrifying could wait for three years or more.

It's a good system. When my oldest son returned home from Micronesia, he was full of stories about spearfishing in the company of curious sharks. Two years had passed since then, so hey, hey. He regaled me with a tale about crossing 200 miles of open ocean in a rowboat-sized craft powered by an unreliable outboard motor. That was a two-years story, too.

Killdeer chick © Doug Parrott

He waited an additional year before he told me about the time he visited an unfriendly island, where the natives disliked outsiders so much they dredged a new island out in the lagoon for the strangers to stay on. One night, a man got drunk and began to shoot at the strangers—including my son—in the middle of the lagoon. "But you shouldn't worry that I was in any danger at all," said my son. "I went to the complete opposite end of the island away from that guy, where I was safe."

It took my son seven more years to tell me that the total length of his island haven was less than 30 meters. Oy.

In our family, we have a Thanksgiving tradition I am very fond of. Before our big meal of the day, we go around the table, and each of us says out loud what he or she is most grateful for. Last year, Alex said this: "I am grateful that in this family, we support each other unconditionally and try to help each other achieve our dreams."

He went on to talk about the fact that some of his fellow Marines in combat in Iraq and Afghanistan lacked such unconditional support from home. They carried, instead, the burden of knowing their folks were terrified by their choice to fight for their country and place themselves in harm's way. But not Alex. He said that instead, he had the privilege of knowing his family supported his choice to take risks, and thus he could do so with a happy heart.

It was one of the best compliments we have ever received, ranking right up there with the one my youngest son paid us when he came home for Thanksgiving after his first quarter of college. "My friends all tell me I have the best parents in the world," he said. But there was a note of puzzlement in his voice. "So I guess you guys must be better than I thought."

A mom can't ask for more than that.

12. Bird Brains and Other IQs

"Did you see anything good at the Fill today?" my husband asked as I shut the door behind me and began to shed layers of clothes like a snake working on a new skin. It's been an icy spring, and I was blue with cold, but mere cold wouldn't stop me from going to my favorite place on Earth.

John always asks me this question when I come home, and I always answer the same way: Yes. One of the greatest charms of the Fill is that there is always something new and exciting to see.

"Today I found Pa Eagle swimming in the lake," I said. Ma and Pa Eagle have been getting ready to lay two eggs in their nest. This is something they've done each year since they moved their nest site to Talaris, the think tank across the street from the Fill. Ma and Pa are experienced parents who have managed to raise five babies in the past three years.

Ma usually lays her eggs in March, but prior to that, she begins sprucing up the nest she uses year after year. It's her version of spring cleaning. Like most males, Pa is willing to help around the home if he gets strong enough signals from his mate. I don't know exactly what signal Ma uses to persuade Pa to get cracking. When I want John to do something around our home, I give him the Look. John says whenever I give him the Look, he feels like going right out and collecting a few twigs.

Bald Eagle calling to its mate © Tim Kuhn

That's exactly what Pa has been doing for the past few weeks. He's not just helping with the cleaning. Like a lot of homeowners, the eagles seem to believe they can always add on a little more—so Pa can often be seen clutching a new stick as he flies back to the nest, having wrenched off a branch from one of the many cottonwood trees in the neighborhood. He presents this token to Ma, who then carefully arranges it to her liking.

Lately, Pa has taken on the added challenge of bringing Ma a lot more food than she can normally catch for herself. She's eating for three, you know. The other day, Pa was swooping back and forth over a hapless coot in the lake. The coot refused to get caught very quickly, so Pa had to work himself almost to exhaustion before he finally managed to grab the coot and carry it away to his favorite eating perch. Before he could lug himself that far, though, Ma showed up and gave a peremptory cry. In midair, Pa turned over and offered up his catch to her. She glided above him and delicately picked the coot from his talons. Then without a backward glance, she flew back to the nest. Meanwhile Pa, beak open and tongue hanging, flapped wearily over to the canoe house to recover.

This morning, Pa was again out hunting for gifts to give Ma. This time he caught a large Double-crested Cormorant. The cormorant had been diving for fish about 50 meters from shore and had apparently believed it was too big for an eagle to bother with. Pa swooped down, stabbed with his claws, and held the cormorant underwater until it drowned. Pa then tried to lift the cormorant out of the water, but he couldn't do it. The cormorant really was too big. Pa floated in the lake for a while like a giant duck, figuring out what to do. Letting go of the cormorant was evidently not an option, for he began to paddle with his wings in a beautiful butterfly stroke that would have made Michael Phelps swoon with envy. He was heading for the mud island that has sprung up from the middle of Waterlily Cove.

I call this island Atlantis because every summer it sinks into the depths of the lake, disappearing as though it had never been. I suppose, though, it would be more accurate to call it "New, Improved Atlantis" because, unlike its namesake, it keeps coming back again each winter. No one knows why the island behaves this way. When it reappears, the birds quickly make use of it as a roost. That's what Pa was planning to do.

The mud island was at least 70 meters away, however, and Pa's wings were heavy with water. I wondered if his determination outweighed his common sense. But he stroked gamely on and on until at last he dragged himself and his prize out onto land.

Ma came winging in for her gift. Then she discovered Pa had brought her a cormorant. Maybe she had been anticipating a tasty coot, or perhaps a plump wigeon. Certainly not a greasy cormorant. With a high-pitched cry, she turned up her beak and flew off.

"Typical, typical," John murmured when I told him this story. "What happened next?"

Giving John a short but piercing version of the Look, I said, "Pa ate the cormorant himself."

John nodded. Clearly that's just what he would have done in similar circumstances. "I bet that's the last time Pa tries to catch a cormorant," he said feelingly.

It was not an idle remark. Eagles, like all hunters, must learn from their mistakes. They aren't endowed with hunting skills upon birth, except perhaps with the basic concept that they must catch things to survive. Dennis Paulson, that great ornithologist and teacher, told my master birder class that he believes hunting may be why raptors, loons, grebes, and other fish-eating birds require as long as four years to mature. If you make your living from hunting, you need to develop enough game-catching skills to reliably bag enough food for yourself and for the babies who will depend on you. Otherwise, no use breeding.

To develop skill, you have to be able to learn from both your mistakes and your successes. You need to be able to assess what works, what doesn't, and *why*, so you can apply the right lessons to future hunting expeditions. Maybe bird brains are much brainier than we think.

This is certainly true for Black-capped Chickadees, for example, who (science now tells us) grow new brain cells every fall and winter so they can remember where they store all the seeds they gather. Imagine how useful it would be to have a chickadee brain—never again would I forget where I last put the remote, an absolutely essential piece of equipment without which I cannot vegetate in front of the TV and yet which gets lost so often I imagine it must grow legs at night and scuttle to some new hiding place.

We humans need to apply even more meaning to life than do birds. This is because our natural habitat is to a large extent each other, and people create very complicated ecologies. In order to make reliable choices about survival in our environment, we need to understand how and why complex systems and even more complex individuals behave the way they do.

This was brought home to me one day after I had moved to Los Angeles to take a new job. An acquaintance and I hit it off at an office party, and after a while, she said, "Oh, we must do lunch."

Not realizing this was the L.A. way of saying "We've had a pleasant conversation," I hauled out my date-book and said, "When would you like to meet?" I thought my new "friend" really wanted to get together for lunch. She thought I was nuts. Neither one of us knew what the other meant.

Eventually, I learned the lingo of L.A., and things became much clearer. Even in Los Angeles, if you try hard enough, you can learn why people behave the way they do.

Nature is a lot more difficult to understand. You can learn the "what" of nature by studying science, but you cannot learn the "why." That's because nature does not have a brain or a heart, so it's hard to figure out what nature means when it acts.

In reality, nature means nothing. It cannot do anything on purpose. It cannot love us or hate us. At the core of the world is a molten slug of iron, not a thinking, feeling, persuadable brain, or a kind and loving heart. Yet indifferent, unfeeling nature acts upon us nevertheless. We get attacked by a bacterium and some of us die, but others don't, or others don't get attacked at all. We trip on a piece of wood and sprain an ankle, or we break a leg, or we skip away with no harm done. We take our hard-earned money down to the 7-Eleven to buy lottery tickets every week and watch the lotto sucker suck out eight ping-pong balls with numbers on them, but the numbers aren't ours. Meanwhile, lazy Joe down the street just won a pile.

These are very deep mysteries, as I discovered during an interview my writing students did with a survivor of the Bataan Death March. After listening for a harrowing hour and a half, one of the kids asked, "What do you make of it all?"

The man had had nearly 60 years to think about it. "I don't know what to make of it," he answered. "Good people lived, and good people died. Bad people lived, and bad people died. It was just random. And you can't build your life on 'random.'"

I've since wondered, "Why not?" Certainly both the natural world and the human-built one are loaded with randomness. Not totally, of course. The world is governed by very real laws, but chance also plays a part. Since this is true, why do we humans insist on trying to assign meaning to everything? Wouldn't it be more rational—maybe even healthier—to accept the world as it is?

The answer is emphatically no. When our brains got big enough to start figuring out complexity—in other words, when we developed the ability to reason—we also developed the desire to apply reason to everything. You can see the advantages of this. A reasoning creature can plan ahead, avoid future pitfalls, control events. If you're a critter without big fangs, sharp talons, or fast running shoes, you need to be able to foresee danger. Otherwise, by the time you get into trouble, it's too late.

Once we started down the path of reason and braininess, though, we couldn't seem to stop. At some point in the process, we became self-aware. "I am, I cried," as Neil Diamond puts it. We became individuals, and as individuals, we began to care about making a difference in the world. We developed the need to *matter*. For us to be happy now, our lives have to mean something.

Unfortunately, this desire for meaning flies in the face of the reality of randomness. How can we apply meaning to events that sometimes just happen to us, wrecking our happiness, wrecking our

Bald Eagle cleaning its talons after a meal © Tim Kuhn

lives? "Things happen for a reason," we often say at such moments, but really we have no clue what it all means.

In my search for meaning, I turn—paradoxically—to uncaring nature. Nature has no heart, no love to offer me. But it does have meaning. Nature connects me to something larger than myself. Nature is eternal. Because it will go on into the future long after I am gone, the tiny mite that I am and the little bit that I can contribute will go on as well. My life will make a difference.

Even more important for me in the here-and-now, where I spool out my days, nature is beauty made real. And that makes me happy—for no particular reason!

"There is no ugly creature," my 97-year-old aunt told me one day. "Most people think some animals are ugly—rats, for instance. But rats are perfectly good animals that are well suited to their environment."

"What about mosquitoes?" I asked, thinking to trip her up.

"Even mosquitoes are beautiful," she replied.

As I opened my mouth to argue, she went on, "I don't like the way they bite and make me itch, but that has nothing to do with whether they are beautiful. If you look at even a mosquito closely enough and understand it well enough, you will see its beauty."

Back at the Fill, as I scratched my latest beautiful mosquito bite, I remembered my aunt and the difference she has made in my life. A quiet woman, shy and humble, she would have classified herself as one of the little people. But oh, how she mattered.

Just as I turned for home, Pa Eagle swooped into Paulson Prairie, lowered his massive talons, and hit the ground. There was an explosion of grass and dirt. Then Pa lifted off, clutching a fistful of soft grass to take back to Ma, almost like a bouquet for their bower.

In the nest, I know, lie two eggs. Eventually, the eggs will hatch, and two new eagles will greet the world. Ma and Pa will get really busy then, bringing fish and coots and ducks to feed the chicks. In July, the youngsters will be too big to fit in the nest anymore. They will stand on the edge, flapping their wings to build strength, crying loud cries to encourage their frazzled parents to bring them more to eat, right now now now.

Even at the height of this stage of life, when the babies are as big as the adults and require almost a conveyor belt of constant food, Pa will sometimes steal a moment from his hunting, dive down into Paulson Prairie, and bring back some grass for Ma. The youngsters will watch intently as Ma takes the grass and arranges it in the nest.

The eaglets will know then that this is what eagles do. In their own time, they will bring such gifts and arrange them just so, and show their own youngsters.

Beauty through the ages. It is enough.

Mock Orange © Doug Parrott

Tree Swallow © Doug Parrott

13. Turn Backward, O Time in Your Flight

Joy lies in the connections we make—with each other and, for me, most of all with nature. Yesterday was a day of pure joy, and all on account of the swallows who welcomed me into their world. Swallows are fast-flying birds who make their living by rocketing around catching insects in the air. They are summer birds at the Fill, and they have been gradually arriving from their homes in the south since February. They're here now in numbers.

We host four resident species: Tree Swallow, Violet-green, Cliff, and Barn. All four were swirling around the Alder Grove near the kiosk yesterday. There must have been a bug hatch in the tall grass that borders the grove, because more than a hundred swallows showed up for the swirl. All of them stayed low, nearly brushing the tops of the grass stalks as they flew. They skimmed the earth at incredible speed, around and around the grove, a living carousel that sang little songs as they worked.

I set down my camp stool in the middle of the swarm, an obstacle in the flight path, but not a significant one. The swallows simply rode a roller-coaster of air up over my head and then back down again to the grass. Many gave me a beady-eyed look as they slid by, and every now and then one would let out a squeak. As far as I could tell, the squeaks aimed at me were no different than the squeaks they gave each other, which seemed to be a kind of sonic traffic control system that prevented anyone from colliding. I began to look forward to each squeak, as a tiny body flew by. I'm not tiny, nor can I fly, but being involved in the squeak fest made me feel I was a part of the birds' world, a kind of stationary, somewhat irritating object perhaps, but accepted.

The swallows took me right back to my childhood, when I would stand watching the carved wooden horses of the Seattle Center's carousel prance around and around in an endless parade of elegance. My favorite horse was a wild black one with tossing mane and flaring tail. I liked him best because he was the fastest—or at least so it seemed to me, despite the fact that his wooden hooves were attached to the platform the same as all the other steeds. What does reality matter to a child with an imagination?

I was that child again yesterday, as the swallows flowed around me, drawing me into their magical merry-go-round, singing and swooping. As I turned one last time to follow their flight, a black shape shot past me. It was a Vaux's Swift, a bird even faster and sleeker than the swallows. The wildest one. The fastest. My favorite.

This ability birds have to create childlike wonder is one of the most enthralling aspects of wild nature. For to a child, all the world is a wonder worth stopping for. We adults have forgotten the child's ability to stop and wonder. We have replaced wonder with purpose.

I noticed this one day at Woodland Park Zoo while I was watching a toddler and his mom approach the lion exhibit. "Let's go see the lions," said the mom, gently dragging her child by the hand toward a set of stairs the zoo folks had thoughtfully installed for the short among us. But instead of climbing up the stairs, the child stopped to look at a mud puddle in the path. The puddle was limned with ripples of iridescent rainbows, the result of a gasoline leak by some passing zoo vehicle. In the sunlight, the rainbows were beautiful, and the kid wanted to examine them up close and personal. Stopping dead in his tracks, he crouched down for a better look, jerking his mother to a sudden stop. The mother waited briefly for her son to finish with the puddle, but the kid wasn't budging. "Dear," she said, tugging on his hand, "look at the lions." The kid pretended not to hear. "We're here to see the lions," the mom gritted out, tugging harder. The kid resisted. In exasperation, the mom lifted the kid bodily away from his puddle and swung him onto the stairs. "There," she said, triumphantly, "there are the lions." Whereupon the kid protested by throwing a tantrum. "The terrible twos," the mother muttered, and hurried her squalling son away from the staring mob.

When I told this story to Marietta Rawson, an expert in early childhood education and the founder of Northwest Montessori School, she laughed. "The mom was there for the purpose of seeing lions," she said. "The child was there for no purpose at all, unless you could say it was for the purpose of seeing whatever the world had to offer."

To a child, Rawson said, everything in the world is new, and everything is equally interesting to explore. "Young children are all scientists," she said, explaining they have to examine and experiment with everything in order to figure out how to function in a world governed by a host of natural and human laws.

It's true. If you watch toddlers at work, you can see they want to learn everything they can about how the world behaves, and since they lack experience with the world, everything must be explored. What happens when you drop a hammer? It falls down, every time. That is how gravity works. If you spill a cup of water, the water flows over everything, getting it wet. That is how flow physics works. If you throw a bowl of spaghetti off your high-chair tray, your mom gets red in the face, especially if this is the third or fourth time you have performed the experiment. Thus is sociology born.

We adults have already learned the basic scientific concepts, says Rawson, and can now make the world (or at least some of it) perform according to our desires. Adults are thus most interested in purpose.

I see this all the time at the Fill. Adults come here in droves to *do* something. Many come to jog. Their purpose is to lose weight or get in shape. Others come through here because they're on their way to somewhere else. Their purpose is to get to a job on campus or to a football game in the stadium. A lot of people come with their dogs. Their purpose is to give their pets a chance to get some fresh air and poop outdoors. One woman brings her dog in a station wagon, which she parks along the fence south of Corporation Yard near the Youth Farm. She opens the back door of her car, lets the dog loose, and hauls out three little white fences, which she lines up on the gravel. Then she tells her dog to jump over the fences. Being a border collie, the dog is happy to oblige. Its purpose is to please its master; her purpose is to train the dog to be a good fence-jumper.

My ostensible purpose at the Fill is to find birds. But really, I come here to find wonder. I am never disappointed so long as I remain open to whatever wonderful thing presents itself.

Last night was a perfect example. John and I went looking for poorwills. Common Poorwills are small, nocturnal birds mostly of eastern Washington, who come out of hiding when it's full dark. They lurk at the sides of roads, looking up into the night sky with their big eyes, searching for moths and beetles flying against the stars. When the poorwills see such a bug, they burst forth from the road, open their wide mouths, and scoop up their prey.

The poorwills are starting their migration now. At least, I think they are. Their habits are not too well known because they operate almost entirely at night. During the day, these birds roost in trees or on the ground, so well camouflaged by their brown, black, and white feathers that they might as well be invisible.

Nobody knows how often they frequent the Fill. The only time one has ever been seen here was in May 2006, when two birders found a stray migrant at midnight. I have a feeling poorwills are more common than that, but who is ever awake and abroad in the dead of night at the Fill to find them?

Well, we are. At least whenever we can manage to stay awake long enough to greet the night. At our age, John and I find that Mr. Sandman usually comes by our house around 7 p.m. and coshes us over the head. Next thing we know, we're sawing lumber. But not last night. Last night, we stayed conscious until full dark had spread its velvety shadow over the Fill. The air was still, and moths began flying up from the still-warm road that runs beside the horsetail wetlands and cattail marshes leading to the Dime Lot. Conditions were perfect for finding poorwills.

The way you find poorwills is by driving very, very slowly along a road, with your headlights on. The headlights catch the eye-shine of the poorwills crouching by the roadside. The eye-shine is exactly the color of a candle lit inside a jack-o'lantern on Halloween—a kind of unearthly orange glow. I have seen this glow three times in my life while birding in eastern Washington, and I want to see it again, only this time at my favorite place on Earth.

So there we were in full dark, with our little hopes up. We were on a treasure hunt! John drove while I sat on the edge of my seat, binoculars at the ready, heart beating wildly from the excitement of the hunt. We held to a steady 3 mph, cruising up the roads and back, scanning for orange glow. Scanning for any glow, actually. Every beer can gave us a jolt, until we saw the glow was cold silver, not molten orange. We searched for 45 minutes until...

...we grew too tired from the excitement to continue. We never did find a poorwill, but I discovered that didn't matter. What we found instead was the long-forgotten, childlike sense of anticipation—the kind that makes you almost forget to breathe. Time turned backwards, and we were ten years old again, out at night without our parents in tow, hunting for treasure, half-believing in magic, feeling leprechauns—or poorwills!—were very near, if only we could see them.

In years past, we would probably have been disappointed at not finding the figurative poorwill pot at the end of the rainbow. But last night, wrapped in the memories of childhood, we found treasure more real: the ability to look beyond an artificial, adult goal and find the joy of just being alive.

14. The Happy Warrior

Mr. Hissy's chicks hatched out yesterday, and now they're tumbling all over themselves down at East Point, eating the lush grasses that grow in the shade of the cottonwood trees. They look like yellow tennis balls with legs, a far cry from their stately parents, a pair of Canada Geese.

Mr. Hissy is one of the many nonmigratory, non-native geese that have found a home here at the Fill, much to the dismay of the UW's Athletics Department. The baseball and soccer players don't like the fact that so many geese make deposits on their fields every day. They've tried a variety of methods to discourage the geese, including hiring a falconer to fly his Peregrine Falcon back and forth over the fields. They've also paid a gunman to shoot off whistling shells from time to time. The raptor and the rifleman are supposed to scare the geese so much that they abandon their feeding grounds and head for safer, quieter climes. Neither threat has worked. The geese, whose weight ratio compared to a falcon is on the order of a dumpster to a bathroom wastebasket, were totally blasé about their would-be predator. They looked up when the falcon coursed past, assessed the risk as zero, and calmly went back to feeding and food processing. The whistling shells worked pretty well at first, but it didn't take the geese long to realize they were all sound and no fury. And so back to business.

In the spring each year, the Canadas become even bigger pests as they change from normally docile creatures into angry bullies. It's breeding season, and the hormones race through their veins

Mr. and Mrs. Hissy © Doug Parrott

and make them aggressive. I've seen male geese chase grown men halfway across the Fill on a good day. But none of the geese I've seen over the years was more aggressive than Mr. Hissy. Mr. Hissy was in a class by himself.

He first came to my attention one day in March when he and the missus decided to establish their nest at East Point. East Point, you should know, is one of the prime overlooks at the Fill. It commands a sweeping view of Lake Washington west as far as the shellhouse, all the way to the lake's eastern shore, and south across Union Bay to Foster Island. It's one of the best spots to check for deep-water rarities such as Long-tailed Ducks and Red-necked Grebes.

So I was quite dismayed when the Canada Goose pair took over the site for the season. I knew there would be no going down to East Point to bird as long as the parents were nesting. In fact, Mr. Hissy was so aggressive that he didn't even let me walk on the path that skirts the point. Mr. Hissy had decided that he needed a no-walk zone of at least 50 meters all around his nest.

The first I knew there was a problem was when I set up my camp stool at the overlook one March morning. No sooner did I raise my binoculars to scan the lake for ducks and grebes than Mr. Hissy came charging out of the cattails straight for me. His horrible pink mouth was agape, his tongue was sticking out, and he was hissing like a radiator about to blow a gasket. The missus stood back a few feet and egged him on, throwing her head up and down and honking encouragement to her brave mate. Without a second to lose, I snatched up my camp stool and fled.

That evening when John came home from work, I told him about being chased by a goose. "I'm not going to be able to look out over the lake for weeks now," I mourned.

"We'll just see about that," my hero replied.

The next day, John accompanied me on my walk. When we got near East Point, we could see the Canada Goose was already on patrol, waddling back and forth across the trail. "Stand back," John told me. Then he straightened up as tall as he could stand, puffed out his chest, and strode toward the goose. "Come on, you big bully, see what it's like to take on a man!" shouted John, beckoning the goose to battle.

This behavior completely baffled the goose at first. I could see that he wanted to attack, but he wasn't sure about the danger this tall, gesticulating hominid presented. He hissed in frustration. "Yeah," taunted John, "you want some of this? Who's bad? Not so feisty now, are you? Go ahead and hiss, Mr. Sissy-Hissy."

I'm not sure exactly what happened next. I was laughing so hard I was crying. From John's description, the goose simply deflated and slunk back into the cattails, leaving John the clear victor. My knight in shining armor strutted back to me, wrapped his arm around my waist, and we continued down the path.

But not for long. Just as John was bragging about his victory, there was a kind of whooshing noise from behind us, and POW! Mr. Hissy struck John's head in a stealth flyby. Then, without stopping to see how *hors* his rival was from *de combat,* the goose disappeared back into the cattails, honking all the way.

There was a long silence. John and I walked on down the path, both deep in thought. Finally, John said, rubbing his head, "You know, the Fill is home for all these birds—we're just casual visitors. Maybe you should skip going to the point for a few days. It would be the kind and generous thing to do."

Thus spake the true alpha male, a guy who can see past the immediate brawl and realize it takes a big man to be willing to concede territory to a fellow creature who needed it far more than we did. The goose was defending his family; we were defending only our fun. In such a contest, a true chevalier gives ground gracefully.

Dominance battles such as this one are not confined to goose-husband confrontations, of course. They are a common and interesting aspect of all of human nature. We do seem to need to know who stands above us and who below. Oh, we may talk about how we are all created equal, but the fact is, we compare ourselves to others all the time. We notice when someone has a higher salary than we do, or a better figure. In school we compete against each other for higher grades or hotter dates. We like to beat each other at poker or watch in the stands while the home team outscores our rivals. Knowing which rung of the ladder we occupy gives us the feeling we know our place in the world, and that knowledge is somehow comforting.

Real happiness, however, cannot come from such comparisons, for while there will always be people we outstrip and who thus make us feel superior, there will also always be those who pass us by and make us feel terrible. If everyone I happen to encounter today falls into the first category, well, what I great day I am having. But it's a fearful day, too, because deep down I know I can come across a person in the second category at any time, and then my happy little day will be ruined.

Living the life comparable thus robs us of security. Furthermore, even if we climb to the top of the ladder and there are no rungs higher, how long can we expect to stay balanced there? The hierarchies we experience today are not the same ones we will experience tomorrow. The ladder is slippery, and no one stays on a comfortable rung for long. I may have mastered every intellectual challenge that crossed my path when I was young and had all my marbles, but as I approach the gray years of my life, I feel lucky when I can remember where I parked the car. So who's the smart one now? The physical beauty that graces youth fades, as does bodily strength. At age 21, I could work all day and all night without sleeping. Why, I could run a marathon. By age 61, I can barely stay awake past 7 p.m., and hundred-yard dashes are threatening to become 20-yard dodders. Nothing can protect us from these realities, not even great wealth. If our happiness depends on such things, we are doomed to grief.

To lead a happy life, we must instead measure our worth against an inner standard, and that standard should be defined in a way that gives us satisfaction. Sigmund Freud defined his standard of happiness as "to work and to love." That's pretty good.

In my own life, I ask myself, was I a kind person today? Did I do something nice for the people I love and for the world I am dedicated to help? Was I cheerful in the face of physical infirmity? Did I care for the environment? These are the yardsticks by which I measure my worth; I am happiest when I succeed in meeting them.

Luckily for me, John shares many of the same values. He may have squared off in a losing battle against Mr. Hissy at first, nose to beak, but when I told him a short while later that I had seen Mrs. Hissy shepherding three yellow goslings into the field to graze, my mate was as proud as hers was to have played a role in the event. He straightened up and nodded his head with satisfaction. I almost expected him to honk.

What a guy.

Canada gosling © Doug Parrott

15. Think Small

It is always a happy day when the Vaux's Swifts return in spring to the Fill. Vaux's Swifts are cigar-shaped, avian missiles equipped with long, pointy wings. They are among the fastest of birds, with an easy cruising speed of 30 miles per hour and the capability to raise that speed to mach 10 when they turn on their turbojets (or at least, so it seems to me, rooted to the ground as I am). Swifts spend nearly all their time in the air, catching insects on the fly, mating in the sky, soaring in the heavens for the sheer fun of flight.

This year, the swifts returned on April 30, a week later than usual. It has been a cold spring, and perhaps the swifts knew to wait in the south till our weather warmed up enough to encourage insects to hatch. Now that the swifts are here, they can be seen every day catching bugs over the fields and groves of the Fill.

The best time to see swifts is not at first light in the early morning. Swifts like to sleep in, I suppose because they must wait for the midmorning sun to warm up their insect prey. Swifts sleep inside chimneys. They don't perch on branches as other birds do—their feet, legs, and stiff tails are adapted instead to cling to vertical surfaces, like tiny woodpeckers. At night, they seek out a disused chimney, which they encircle in an ever-tightening cyclone of birds. Then, at some unseen signal, the swifts begin to dive into the chimney.

The chimney at St. Stephen's Church three-quarters of a mile from the Fill hosted swifts for a few years, but eventually either the chimney changed or the swifts did, and they no longer swarm there at night. I've heard rumors that the swifts now roost in a home-owner's chimney somewhere else in the neighborhood. It would be fun to go on a chimney hunt one of these evenings, following the swifts home.

This morning, the swifts' insect prey must have hatched out of the grass around the Wedding Rock because the birds were swooping low along the ground there. Usually Vaux's Swifts fly higher than the treetops, flashing by so fast and so far away, it is hard to study any one individual. But today, swifts were flying by at my level. I set up my camp stool in the middle of their flight path and became an instant insect magnet. Little gnats began swarming all around me, creating a kind of Pigpen-like aura of flavorful bugs. (Pigpen, you may recall, was the Peanuts cartoon character who carried a swirling dust cloud with him wherever he went.)

The swifts, attracted by my smorgasbord, began flying closer and closer. I could hear the wind they made as they whooshed by. Other birds make a whistling noise when they fly, the result of wind flowing past their feathers. Swifts, I now know, make their own wind, an altogether different sound. It was enchanting, almost as enchanting as the look each bird gave me as it rocketed past, sharing a glance as we shared the day.

A friend of mine once asked me, "How *exactly* do you connect with nature?" He had often heard me spout off about the pleasure I get when I make that connection, but he had been unable to plug in. He wanted a how-to.

"Well," I said slowly, never having written down a recipe, "I guess I try to enter the birds' world. If I am patient, and if the birds are willing, sometimes they will let me in, and we can share a part of their world. We make a connection by sharing."

He went away satisfied, but I was not. How can I share the birds' world when I am so different from them? I can't fly and will never know the glorious feeling of soaring and sinking under my own power. Yet flying defines the very lives of aerialists such as Vaux's Swifts. How can I hope to enter their world when I am denied the greatest part of it?

Many years ago, my husband bought me hang gliding lessons for my birthday because he thought I needed to be more adventurous.

Orange-crowned Warbler ©Gregg Thompson

Hang gliding was the last thing I wanted to do, but we were so poor in those days, and the lessons were so expensive, it seemed a sin to waste the money he had spent. So I went. The instructor outfitted us with a harness and a hang glider, moved us to the edge of a sandy cliff, and told us to jump off. The next thing I knew, I was face-planted in the sand, having soared for a total of five feet before plunging to my doom. As I lay there, wondering how many bones I had broken, I heard the instructor come flying down the cliff. He was yelling.

"Oh good," I thought, "he is concerned about my welfare and is trying to find out if I'm still alive." But no. When he got close enough, I discovered he was yelling about his hang glider and how much I would regret it if I had damaged it. That was the last time I tried to fly like a bird.

Flying is not the only door closed to me. I can't sing like a bird. I have no feathers. I don't lay eggs or brood chicks, nor do I produce a new bunch of kids every year, thank goodness. I am protected from the environment by the artifacts of my culture, so I don't have to endure bad weather unless I choose to. No one tries to hunt me or steal my food. The list goes on and on. My 97-year-old aunt used to say, "You can never understand a phase of life until you live through it yourself." If that is true, then I will never truly understand—much

Wild Rose © Doug Parrott

less, share—the lives of the birds I love so much to watch.

Thinking these thoughts, I ambled down the Loop Trail and set up my camp stool in one of my favorite spots at the Fill: the bend in the trail near Kern's Restoration Pond. This is a place so shielded by native brush and trees that almost all the traffic noise from the floating bridge is blocked out. It is a quiet little sanctuary, where the birds often come into the open. There is so much cover here that even the shyest bird can feel confident about its safety. The tranquility of nature is broken only by the occasional jogger, baby walker, or birder, people who soon pass on to more open vistas.

I settled down to await developments. Within a matter of minutes, the leaves on a wild rose bush rustled a little, and I knew a bird was getting near. I could track its progress by the rustling trail it made in the bush. When the bird reached the edge of the bush, it popped up into view: an Orange-crowned Warbler, mere inches from my face.

Orange-crowned Warblers are our dullest wood-warbler, a bird so plain its field marks are defined more by their absence: no distinct color, no wing bars, no outstanding markings of any kind. "Dingy," says Roger Tory Peterson in his book *Western Birds.* The bird's name has always been a mystery to me. Orange crown? Sounds like its head feathers would be on fire. But from what I've seen, an Orange-crowned Warbler's crown is just as dull as the rest of the bird.

Until today. Today, as the bird bowed its little head to search for an insect among the leaves, the sun came out and lit up its feathers. Nestled among the dull olive on its head were orange plumes so subtly colored as to blend in almost completely with the green. How is it possible for orange and olive to look so similar? Beats me, but the bird's head was aglow with the subtle combination of these two colors. The feathers seemed to shimmer and change place with each movement of the bird's head, like iridescent silk that looks now one color, now another. The bird kept glancing at me as it foraged, and the realization came to me:

It is not only in the sharing that we open ourselves to nature, but also in the noticing of every small detail.

We don't see with our eyes alone, like a camera shooting a subject at a focal length of x, an exposure of y, and a focus of z. We see with our minds. We take in all the world's information through our senses, yes, but we *notice* with our minds. The more we notice, the more meaningful and powerful the impact becomes.

When I noticed that a Vaux's Swift makes its own wind, and the sound that wind makes is different from any other sound I have ever heard, that is when I entered the bird's world. Through my senses, but with my mind. When I noticed the Orange-crowned Warbler's feet clutching a leaf stem, and saw how its sharp claws overlapped each other, giving the bird an unbreakable grip on its quivering perch, I entered this one little part of its world. Now I understand how an Orange-crowned Warbler manages to hold on so hard it can bend its head down to eat and show me its breathtaking crown.

The old adage "Stop and smell the roses" became clear. Yes, we should take the time out of our busy days to smell the occasional rose. But that isn't what the adage is really telling us to do. Rather, we must stop a while if we are to notice this one small aspect of the rose. Noticing takes time, effort, and thought. To notice something, we must stop whatever else we're doing. We have to focus on one thing, use our senses to identify its color, smell, feel, taste. Then we have to think at least one thought.

I think thoughts like these: I wish I could fly like a swift. I wonder if I would rather have wings or hands. It sure took me a long time to see the orange crown of an Orange-crowned Warbler. I wonder how many bugs a warbler has to eat before it feels full. The whoosh of the cars on the bridge is ugly, but the whoosh of a swift is beautiful.

It doesn't matter what thought you think. When you're noticing nature, a deep thought is as good as a dumb one. The point is to notice consciously. When you notice the small things, you enter nature's world because small is accessible, manageable, within reach. When you notice any detail of nature's wonder, a window opens. You can poke your head out that window and discover that you are a part of nature, too.

We are connected.

16. Fear

Fear stalks me. At night, it comes after me in my dreams. Sometimes it takes the shape of a faceless man, looming over me like doom itself. Other times—worse times—it's a Warg, the fearsome, wolf-like mount of the Orcs in Tolkien's *Lord of the Rings.* When it chases me, sometimes I turn and fight it. Those are good morning-afters, because I know if I can handle fear, I can handle everything else. More often, though, I run and run, fear at my heels, grabbing at my clothes. (On a lighter note, at least in these nightmares I am still wearing clothes! I don't know how it is with men, but it turns out that women commonly dream about the embarrassment of appearing in public half-clothed, or less.) On rare occasions, fear catches me. When that happens, I bolt awake, sweating and shaking.

My son has gone to war, and I am afraid.

I do not like the telephone to ring, for that is how bad news appears. I do not like the doorbell to sound, for that is how the worst announces itself.

My neighbors know this. One day in the spring, when my door stood open, two of them came over to tell me they had thought hard about how they would contact me in the future. They said, "We decided to stand at your door and shout 'Yoo-hoo!' as loudly as we could. We figured the military would never do that, so you would know it's just us."

The daytime is not as hard as the night. I can push the fear down into the cellar of my soul, where it can lurk but not alarm. Yet I know it is there, in the same place where I am.

American Coots escaping an eagle attack © Kathrine Lloyd

I fear for more than just my son and all the other mothers' sons and daughters in harm's way. I'm afraid when my kids get behind the wheel of a car and drive. Their lack of fear is frightening! I worry when biologists I respect talk about the unceasing expansion of human population and its impact on wildlife. I angst when scientists make predictions about species extinctions and the loss of balance in nature. Over the years at the Fill, I have noticed the decline of bird numbers, especially shorebirds, and that bothers me. I'm scared about the inanity of our leaders, the worldwide strength of fundamentalism, the attacks on the Enlightenment. My worry centers seem to be permanently switched on. I don't like it, but what can I do?

I need an Edna Mode to jump onto my coffee table (as she did for Elastigirl in the animated film *The Incredibles*), swat me on the head a few times with a rolled-up magazine, and shout, "Pull-yourself-together! 'What can I do?' Is this a question? ...Go! Confront the problem! Fight! Win!"

Fear is not all bad. It has many good points, in fact. It alerts us to danger. It helps us prepare against calamity so we can ward it off altogether or weather it when it comes. It makes us think twice about taking risks.

But what happens when fear takes over, banishing reason, empathy, kindness, and light, leaving nothing behind but terror and anger? Captain Kathryn Janeway of Star Trek's *Voyager* said that unreasoning fear exists for only one reason: it exists to be conquered. When my unreasoning fear grows so strong it threatens to choke me, I go to the Fill. I like to set up my camp stool at the far south end of the Loop Trail, where I can gaze out at the water. There, I wait for the eagles.

The Bald Eagles who nest at nearby Talaris come to the Fill every day to hunt for their favorite food, American Coots. The coots huddle along the shoreline or gather in large rafts out on the lake, hoping there is safety in numbers. There is not. The eagles have perfected their hunting technique so well they rarely go back to the nest empty-taloned. Some hapless coot or duck or fish almost always meets its fate, lying limply in the grasp of the eagle as the hunter returns to its roost to feed.

This drama of life and death happens every day at the Fill. The birds aren't playing. Someone is going to die and thus never know the beauty of another dawn, never again know the sound of the wind ruffling the water, the feel of rain sliding off a back, the taste of a fresh lily stem.

Like a Roman circus fan, I watch while the eagle selects its target, swoops back and forth over it, forces it to dive to exhaustion, then plummets down for the final coup. I wonder if the Romans ever experienced the same ambivalence I do: pity for the victim, gladness for the victor.

I notice that after the eagle flies off with its prey, the other coots and ducks quickly settle back down and go on about the business of their lives. Some begin preening. Others upend themselves and dabble for food. The divers plunge underwater and come up with a fish. The wigeons, who often forage in the grassy fields at night, go back to sleep. No one grieves. Life goes on.

Life does go on, doesn't it? When the eagle has passed and the birds resume their activities, I can see again the world is okay. In some sense, the world will always be okay. Nature will go on. No matter what happens to me or mine, no matter how much we humans destroy each other and nature, nature will survive. And because nature will continue and life will go on, whatever we ourselves leave behind will also continue, at least in some small degree.

After my mother died, the rabbi who conducted her funeral service spoke about the Jewish idea of the afterlife. Like many things in Jewish culture, there are different schools of thought about what God has in mind. Some Jews believe the hereafter consists of resurrection: you come back to life as yourself again, only things are much better now because you're living in paradise. Other Jews believe in reincarnation: you come back to this same earthly life, only you're someone or something completely different. My mother wanted to come back as a whale. Her headstone is the only one in the entire Jewish cemetery with a humpback carved on it—a strange-looking, misshapen whale because the carver had never made one before. Some Jews believe you will face judgment after you die: if you did wrong here, you must pay for your misdeeds in the place of punishment. But others say all of us—the good, the bad, and the ugly—are going to the same place, a kind of hell where we have to live together, just as we do here on Earth. Holy mackerel.

Faced with this mishmash of beliefs, our rabbi had to say something that would make sense to everyone in the audience. He said this: No matter what you believe about the afterlife, the people we love live on in us, in our memories and in the ways they influenced us. We in turn pass those experiences and qualities on to those who come into our lives. And thus we achieve a kind of immortality.

I'm not interested in immortality for myself. Frankly, it sounds kind of dull. But I do care deeply about protecting the people and things I love. It is for them I fear most. Whatever happens to me or to them, I believe nothing can take away the fact that we all share in this immortality of the human heart. We do matter. The things we do matter. The world will go on, and we will forever be a part of it.

No fear can prevent. For we are stronger than fear, kinder than evil, better than the dark angels of terror and anger that live in us but cannot reign over us unless we let them.

Lorquin's Admiral © Doug Parrott

Part III
Summer

17. Beyond Our Senses

It must be hard to be a woodpecker. For one thing, all that head-banging can't be very good for your brains. More to the point, how does one even go about finding the right piece of wood to bang your head against? The number of trees and snags in the Fill is large. They can't all have the right insects under their bark.

Luckily, this past week the Downy Woodpecker family that has been nesting in the cottonwoods at Boy Scout Pond staged a demo, and I was privileged to be in the audience. Here's how it's done.

First, mom came roller-coastering out of the woods and landed in a dead snag bordering the marsh. She began banging away at the wood. Soon junior came bouncing out to join her, followed by dad, whose little red topknot gleamed in the weak sunlight. Junior watched intently as mom pecked. Her bill moved so fast it was impossible to see the motion distinctly—only a blur showed in my binoculars. She stopped a few times, as if encouraging her little one to try. But junior was clueless. All three woodpeckers looked baffled for a minute. Then dad tried his beak at the lesson. He flew to another tree and waited till the family had positioned themselves to watch. Then, WHAM WHAM WHAM! Same lesson, just louder.

It is said that woodpeckers can detect their larval prey through sound alone. I find this hard to believe, given the noisiness of the Fill—the constant roar of traffic across the bridge, the drone of a Laurelhurst neighbor's pontoon plane taking off, the shouts of the crew coaches spurring their kids on to greater effort. There is always a lot of noise pollution in a city. How can you hope to hear a sound as tiny as that of a grub inching its way inside the wood of a tree?

But my husband, the physicist, has no trouble believing this tale. "When I was a paperboy in Iowa," he said, "I could always sense when one of my customers was hiding in the house so he wouldn't have to pay me when I came around to collect for delivering his newspapers. I would knock on the door and listen for a body in the room, just like a carpenter knocks against a wall and listens for a stud. If that didn't work, I would knock again and freeze. Somehow, I always knew when my customer was there, standing just behind the door, trying to breathe without a sound. I think I could sense my prey's vibrations through my feet. A paperboy with sensitive feet can go far in this world."

I still don't know if I believe that woodpeckers can hear grubs moving inside wood. But I am willing to concede that beings different from me can have senses and abilities I cannot hope to understand. The other day, for example, a man was out walking his Scottie around the Loop Trail. The dog stopped at a clump of grass and began to sniff. His nose went from blade to blade, then slid up a notch and repeated the process, ratcheting up the ladder, so to speak, until the entire clump was sniffed. Meanwhile, the dog's owner stood by patiently the whole while. When he noticed me watching, he smiled and said, "I hate to disturb anyone who's studying, don't you? I just wish I knew what he was reading!"

I do, too. What a rich world the Fill provides for that dog, loaded with stimuli for his eyes, ears, nose, and skin to sense. The Fill is rich for me, too, but it would be even more wonderful if my nose could enable me to construct a picture of every passing critter, as dogs' can; if my ears could hear in the highest upper register as Brown Creepers' can; if my skin could control every hair separately, the way Ring-billed Gulls can control their feathers.

I guess we humans are compensated for our limited senses by having big brains. We can process data from the outside world and apply meaning to it, gain wisdom from it, tell jokes about it, create fantasies, remember the past, speculate about the future. Woodpeckers can't do that! Too much of their braincase is taken up by a tongue that wraps clear around the inside of the skull.

Female Downy Woodpecker © Doug Parrott

Most of the time, I love my brain and its ability to interpret the world. Every now and then, though, I find myself wishing my brain were even better. When my husband talks to me about his quantum physics theories and asks me to comment on a new graph he has just constructed, I wish my brain had been gifted with more neurons in the numbers drawer. It would be nice to appreciate his work on a deeper level than noticing how pretty are the colors he picked for his latest wave function.

Howard Gardner, professor of cognition and education at Harvard University, says there are nine different kinds of intelligence among humans: numbers smart, people smart, spatial smart, linguistics smart, body smart, musical smart, existential smart, self smart, and nature smart. Gardner doesn't stack these different intelligences into any kind of hierarchy, but he does say of nature smart (my kind of intelligence): "This ability was clearly of value in our evolutionary past as hunters, gatherers, and farmers.... It is also speculated that much of our consumer society exploits the naturalist intelligence, which can be mobilized in the discrimination among cars, sneakers, kinds of makeup, and the like."

Talk about damning with faint praise. Evidently, my kind of intelligence is low on the totem pole, useful when we were living in prehistoric times, but now that we're not, still good for foraging in the mall. In other words, Neanderthal meets Valley Girl. Well, we can't all be Einsteins.

And that is just my point. The great strength of our species is our variability. It is this trait more than any other which has given us the success we enjoy today. This is because for generations, we humans have created our own environment, apart from nature. We wear clothes, construct homes, ride bikes, read books, invent language. It is a built environment we inhabit, one we made for ourselves. And as any deity would tell you, creating an entire environment is hard to do. For us ordinary mortals, it would be impossible without the ability to specialize. Because we can specialize—and delegate—we don't have to do everything ourselves. We can rely on specialized members of our species to do what we ourselves can't.

However, as the dinosaurs found out, specializing too much is risky. You can box yourself into such a small niche that you become unable to adjust to change. This is an especially big danger for those of us who have specialized in ancient skills at the expense of learning new ones. I can change a typewriter ribbon in an Underwood, for example, but I have no idea how to program my TV remote. Makes me feel out of touch with my environment, just as the last pterosaur might have felt, looking at all the new-fangled birds.

One of the biggest new marvels in my lifetime is the interconnectedness of the world. Never in human history have so many different cultures interacted with one another, and so easily—just a few thumb-clicks away for those with texting apps on their cell phones. The potential for rapid change is staggering.

To navigate this new world well, it seems to me we must learn to value—not envy—qualities and abilities that we ourselves do not have. This can be hard to do for creatures such as ourselves, who measure our worth mostly with the yardstick of comparison. The comparisons we make are usually with people who have more than we do, not with those who have less. Americans who earn $25,000 a year, for example, are wealthier than 90 percent of the people on the planet, yet no American who makes $12 an hour feels wealthy. That's because we compare ourselves to people down the street who have a better car or a bigger house. Not even the wealthiest 1 percent of Americans really feel all that privileged. They're too busy noticing that Lord Jones down the boulevard is wealthier still, and everybody knows you have to keep up with the Joneses.

Well, not everybody. When I go to the Fill and see a great bird—which happens every time I go—I feel no one on the planet is richer than I am. Watching the woodpecker family find tasty grubs under tree bark, I marvel at senses that are beyond my ability to match, senses that are even beyond my ken. I don't envy the woodpeckers. On the contrary, whenever I watch the parents try to pass on their bug-finding expertise to their youngster, one thought lies uppermost in my mind: Thank goodness I don't have to whang my head against a tree to be able to value the skill of a woodpecker who does.

18. Snow White

"I used to be Snow White," said Mae West, the Hollywood sex symbol, "but I drifted."

I know just what she means. My own drift to the bad happened the other day down at the Corporation Yards. In my case, it began not with a snake and a piece of fruit but with a Lazuli Bunting and a song. Here's the story.

A few weeks ago, my friend and fellow master birder Evan Houston told me he had seen two male Lazuli Buntings singing a duel behind the greenhouses. Lazuli Buntings are rare anywhere in urban King County and appear almost never at the Fill. They are rural finches with celestial blue heads and backs, cinnamon breasts, and snow-white bellies. Two years ago, two or possibly three males established territory in the fields east of the Corporation Yards and bred, an astonishing event for the Fill. I've been hoping they would return in June and set up housekeeping again. Apparently, according to Evan, the males at least are house-hunting now.

Unfortunately, they have been reluctant to show themselves to me. For the past three weeks at least, I've been scuttling all over the Fill trying to find those darn buntings. Other birders have sent me tantalizing reports of brief sightings: a male north of Main Pond, fly catching and then fleeing; a male singing on top of a compost heap in plain view; two males singing on territory, one at the greenhouses, the other near the Youth Garden. Meanwhile, I've been striking out on the buntings.

Part of my problem is that I am not very skilled at recognizing birds' songs. Lazuli Buntings are related to finches, which have some

Male Lazuli Bunting © Doug Parrott

of the most complex songs in the bird kingdom. To my ear, the males sound like they're singing Hungarian rap: their songs go on and on, there is no identifiable tune (though the music can be pretty), and you can't understand a single word. When Lazuli Buntings sing, their voices just blend into a kind of sound-goulash for me, making them completely indistinguishable from all the other bird songs I hear at the Fill in spring.

After I came home for the 20th time, buntingless and grumpy, my husband finally snapped. "That does it," he said. "I'm going to help you find that bird." He proposed to accompany me to the Corporation Yards the next day, with his computer loaded for bunting. He would play the male's song for me in the car, just before I leapt out to listen near the bunting's territory. His theory was that if I heard the song milliseconds before I entered the field, even my feeble musical skills would enable me to retain the memory long enough to recognize a real bird.

The next morning we put John's theory into practice. We drove over to the Yards and hauled out the computer. John softly played the Lazuli Bunting's song a few times, endeavoring to imprint me. No good. "Please open the windows so I can get a little air," I asked. "Oh, and crank up the sound. I need to hear it better."

John and I have been married for 31 happy years. When you've spent that much time together, you get so you can interpret what

Twinberry © Doug Parrott

your spouse means without the inconvenience of having to be specific. You understand each other subliminally. I've noticed this phenomenon at restaurants when I see 80-year-old couples eating dinner together. They never speak. I used to think this was because they had long ago said everything there was to be said to each other, and now they prefer to subsist in some existential dungeon where physical presence alone is all the contact they want. However, now that my own marriage has passed the 30-year mark, I realize those elderly couples are communicating at a furious rate—they just use telepathy instead of words.

Telepathically interpreting my message correctly, John not only turned up the volume as high as it would go, he stuck his computer out the window and pointed it at Corporation Yard Pond. Within seconds, a male Lazuli Bunting appeared out of nowhere, perched on the hood of our car, looked around for his "rival" for three seconds, and then disappeared into the bushes, never to be seen again.

Recently, the Seattle Audubon Society has been struggling with the ethics of luring in birds by playing recordings of their songs. When male birds arrive on their breeding grounds, they start singing to attract a mate and also to warn rivals to stay away from their territory. If a male hears another male singing nearby, he will usually pop up out of hiding to find the rival bird and drive him off. Birds can't tell the difference between a recording and a rival, so playing their songs will usually attract a male into the open, where he can be viewed by birders.

Playing recordings is controversial. Many people think it is wrong to make a bird respond to such an artificial lure. They worry the male will waste energy trying to find a nonexistent rival, or perhaps he will show himself just in time to be snapped up by a predator. Scientists tell us that for some species, when a male fails to drive off a rival (in this case, the rival being a birder who persistently plays a recording), the females in the area disdain him as ineffectual. The most extreme naturalists believe that disturbing a bird for any reason is wrong because we humans have already deprived birds of so much.

On the other hand, there are birders who say that all birding bothers the birds to some degree, so if you're a birder at all, you're going to have some kind of impact. The question is, does your presence disturb a bird unduly? Usually, the answer is no. Furthermore, say these birders, playing a brief recording doesn't bother the birds significantly either, at least not enough to matter. In fact, recordings might actually save more of the environment because they make a bird come to the birders, thereby encouraging people to stay on a trail or road instead of trampling habitat.

To Aldo Leopold, this modern-day conflict between human needs and birds' needs would come as no surprise. Writing in 1949, he saw that the human need for ever-rising standards of living was eliminating more and more wild lands. Leopold wanted to change the way we think about the natural world and our place in it. In his essay "Land Ethic," Leopold advocated for the elevation of the status of land (by which he meant the biota, as well) to the same philosophical level as human beings. Leopold theorized that if people stopped treating land as property and instead started thinking of it as a living community, we might be more considerate of it. We might, in short, treat it ethically.

For ethics to work, however, Leopold says that people must be willing to acknowledge two things: that other beings have the right to survive, and that we all exist in a community that must cooperate in order to thrive. So when a conflict of interest arises, Leopold would have us ask ourselves not just, "What do I need or want?" but also, "What is best for the community as a whole?"

There is no doubt in my mind that if birds were asked what is best for them, they would not reply, "We think it's okay to play tapes that manipulate us, just as long as you don't do it too much." Similarly, if birds were asked, "Do you mind if people stomp through your habitat and stare at you with gigantic lenses that magnify their eyes to the size of mangelwurzels?" they would answer, "We wish you would just leave us alone."

I do not leave birds alone. I watch them. I tell myself this is okay because I am careful to bother the birds as little as possible. When a bird alights on the path in front of me, I stop and wait for it to do its business and then leave of its own volition. Sometimes I have to wait through an entire dustbath, or a meal, or a preen, but I figure it's the least I can do so as not to disturb the bird.

I don't play recordings, either, or imitate calls to attract birds to me. I prefer to enter nature quietly and patiently, waiting for the birds to accept me into their world and come out where I can see them. Sometimes the birds take a long time to come out. Virginia Rails, for example, are among the shyest birds at the Fill. They often call from deep within the cattails of Southwest Pond, but I see them only rarely. In my early birding days, I would sometimes pick up two pebbles and click them together, imitating the rails' call. Now I take a different approach. If they choose not to appear, well, I tell myself, that's just the way the suet crumbles.

I guess you could sum up my philosophy by saying I follow a kind of birders' Hippocratic Oath, which says in part: First, do no harm. This seems to me to be the most ethical way to bird. On the other hand, I must remind myself of something a friend once said: "Humans are not rational creatures; we are rational*izing* creatures." So maybe I'm just comforting myself with a happy hypocrisy.

After the Lazuli Bunting flew back into the bushes around Corporation Yard Pond, my husband and I sat pondering for a while. I could tell he was feeling guilty about cheating. He could tell I was trying to reconcile my ideals with my behavior. "Man is born to trouble as the sparks fly upward," I quoted to myself. That didn't help. "Nobody's perfect," I continued. Still no help.

"That wasn't very satisfying, was it?" my husband said, interrupting my reverie.

"You mean the fact that we used technology out here in the wild, and we got a bird to land on our car as a result?" I asked. "No, that wasn't exactly my idea of communing with nature."

"Well," said John, "at least he didn't poop on the car." He paused. "I kind of wish he had."

Me, too. Drifting wasn't as fun as Mae West had claimed.

Virginia Rail © Tim Kuhn

19. Birds of a Feather

As much as I seek the similarities between birds and people when I am out in the field, I do know that I am not a bird. I cannot fly. I do not molt or migrate. When my grown children ask to come home for a while to roost, I do not peck or drive them away, as the eagles do.

Do the birds know I am not one of them? That's a bit hard to answer. On the one hand, many of the birds at the Fill are wary of me. The Savannah Sparrows often raise their head feathers in alarm when I come too close to their favorite grass stems. The Killdeer on Shoveler's Pond starts calling the minute it sees my blue hat approach. On the other hand, Savannahs and Killdeers are wary of any big bird. They keep an eye on all us jumbo-sized critters, just in case we should take the notion to eat them.

Lately, the Mallards who are flocking on Main Pond now that breeding season is ending have allowed me to join their flock. Whenever I set up my camp stool at the southern end of the pond, the Mallards begin to float over from the far shore. Eventually, they come out of the water to feed on the weeds all around me. Some snuffle for food in the mud nearby or dabble for plants a little farther out in the water. They bathe or preen. A few even go to sleep.

I sit there enchanted as the ducks ebb and flow. They talk to each other, you know, keeping up a constant commentary. I talk back. "You're looking a little scruffy today," I'll say to one molting male. He doesn't seem to resent my observation. On the contrary, I think the ducks like the sound of my voice. It reassures them that I am settled, unlikely to leap up and grab one of them. Sometimes I'll give

120

a muted quack, just to see if anyone notices. I take care to do this when I'm sure no people are around to hear me. I'm weird enough as it is.

It's amazingly comforting to be in a flock. Like any functional community, the members watch out for each other. They pay attention to what each one is doing. They're interested in what everyone has to say. They don't always get along perfectly—sometimes one duck bites another or chases it around the pond for a while. But they accept each other, too. They all belong, and in a small way, I do too.

I never feel this way in a large flock of people. In crowds, I always worry that someone is going to steal my wallet. My daughter has tried for years to get me to go to large gatherings. She did manage to drag me to a drum circle that formed spontaneously near the fountain at Seattle Center during a Folklife Festival once. While she effortlessly joined the group that was swaying hypnotically to the drumbeat, I stood awkwardly lifting one foot randomly and then another. I was definitely the odd duck out.

And yet even I, a person usually at the far end of the bell curve when it comes to conformity, can appreciate the power of people when they flock together to do something. It is estimated, for example, that the Great Pyramid of Khufu in Giza—the only one of the Seven Wonders of the World still standing—was completed in only 20 years. What a miracle of organization.

"Yes, but the workers were all slaves," said a friend of mine when I was bloviating to her about this. "They had to do exactly what they were told or they would have been punished, maybe killed. What is so miraculous about that?"

But that isn't so. As best we can tell, the Egyptians were paid workers. Whenever the Nile River rose over its banks and flooded the flatlands, which was every spring, the farmers would look to the pharaoh for jobs and food. For the duration of the flood, they would work on the king's pyramid for a daily ration of bread and beer.

Thousands of people were employed on the project, each man doing his assigned job in an orderly progression, as the pyramid rose higher and higher. When it was all done—the pyramid faced with

Male Mallard fluffing his wings © Kathrine Lloyd

shining white limestone and capped with a solid gold pyramidon whose gleam must have been visible for miles—I can easily imagine the pharaoh and the workers all standing back in admiration, totally gratified by what they had accomplished together.

It is one of the greatest strengths of our species that we are capable of cooperating with each other to create something greater than any one of us could ever do alone. I saw this for myself at the 2011 Experimental Nuclear Magnetic Resonance Conference (ENC) at Asilomar in northern California, which my physicist husband John and I attended. The ENC is an annual gathering of brainy folks who work in the field of nuclear magnetic resonance (NMR) imaging. Every year, the prestigious Günther Laukien Prize is awarded at the conference to a physicist whose cutting-edge research advances our understanding of NMR principles. This year, John won, sharing the prize with two scientists from IBM.

As in years past, there were people from nearly every continent and every race at the conference. The men outnumbered the women, but not by very much. There were young scientists just starting their careers, and old scientists finishing theirs. Each person who attended was working on a separate aspect of NMR research. Some were seeking to understand how proteins worked in the body. Others wanted to know how solids could carry more electricity. Some of the scientists were pure theorists. Others were eminently practical.

Chicory © Doug Parrott

One guy from Washington State University was studying how water flows through noodles as they dry. He was helping a food company whose spaghetti noodles kept cracking in the drying process, ruining them for the market.

Everyone, though, talked the same language and wanted to understand each other's work. They were eager to help each other get over obstacles in the path toward greater understanding—of the physical world and of each other.

To me, a nontechnical person who never took a physics class in her life, their talk sounded incomprehensibly like this: "*Wugga wugga wugga,* Zeeman energy. *Wugga wugga,* Hilbert state-space. *Wugga wugga,* Kähler manifold. Thus, *awugga wug.*" I found, though, that if I nodded my head and frowned thoughtfully, people believed I understood every word. They would beam with joy when I showed up at their poster displays to ask them about their work.

I didn't learn any physics from them, but I did learn that they were people united in the goal to enlarge the envelope of human understanding. Like the pyramid builders of old, they were working together to create something lasting and beautiful. And like the Mallards at the Fill, they were willing to let me share in their communal lives, at least a little.

I don't have to be a bird or a physicist to know what a generous gift that was.

20. For Love or Money?

Recently, I shared a morning with a Cinnamon Teal who was guarding the farthest corner of Southwest Pond. Well, perhaps "guarding" is not the right word. "Sleeping on" would be more accurate, for that is all the bird ever seems to do. Cinnamon Teal males are done with breeding by mid-June, leaving their significant others to raise the babies alone. The males have more important work to do: They must change their flamboyant breeding feathers into inconspicuous eclipse plumage that resembles the camouflage of their mates. If you're a tasty duck, it's risky to stand out, so the faster you can fade into the background, the better. The male on Southwest Pond, however, does not seem to be in any hurry to do so. He's still just as mahogany bright as ever, glowing in the late July sunlight.

It's very peaceful spending time with him, he on his tussock and I on my camp stool. I sit as still as he does, dozing only a dozen feet away from him. I'm glad he trusts me enough to let me get so close while he sleeps. He did open one eye when I set up my stool, but when I sat down, his eye closed, and he went back to sleep. Both of us let the calm of the pond flow around us. It is all so familiar: the bagpipe calls of the Red-winged Blackbirds; the cheeps of the baby Tree Swallows in their nest hole, calling whenever a parent arrives with a breakfast bug; the drone of the pontoon plane leaving its berth at a Laurelhurst dock. I guess it is the familiarity that produces the peace. Both the duck and I know every sound is safe, the same way a sailing captain must have known the safe creak of every timber of his tall ship. You'd think all the racket would be noisy, maybe even nervy, but instead it is calming.

Male Cinnamon Teal © Tim Kuhn

I often come to this very spot for the calmness. Even in winter, when my ducky companion has flown south, there is always the Marsh Wren rattling his dry song, the Downy Woodpecker family banging on the dead snags, the House Finches singing their gossip to each other.

The Fill grants me many things. The most thrilling, I have to admit, is the discovery of a rare bird, such as the Brown Thrasher I found this spring, a polka-dotted cinnamon stick of rarity from Indiana or some other Midwest stronghold. What a jaw-dropping surprise—a bird never seen at the Fill by anyone before in more than a hundred years of birding, and only the second one ever found in King County. But such peak moments of joy are not the real reason I try to spend part of every day here. No, it is more for the peace I come, a respite from the stresses and worries I struggle against.

I am not the only one who finds such peace. Many people bring their troubles to the Fill and are comforted. I think it is the promise of eternity we receive. Birds don't live long lives, but nature is ever-renewing. I know my favorite Cinnamon Teal may not be here next year to make me smile at his complacency, but other teals will carry on into the future, just as they have done for thousands of years in the past. Thus, my own troubles fade into the context of a continuous past stretching back as far as I can imagine, and a trustworthy future reaching forward farther than I can see. It is the perspective of the eternal that gives me hope.

When I was a young mother, my two sons were among the worst-behaved babies ever born. One of them routinely began screaming every day at 5 p.m., back stiffened into an arc, face becoming redder by the minute. Nothing I did would soothe him. It was like holding an enpurpled, yelling board. The other one cried pretty much continuously for 18 months. As I staggered through day after day of wailing babies, I could not believe this trying time would ever end.

Now, almost 30 years later, I realize that phase was short. When my kids have their own babies who cry continuously (and karmic justice must, will see that they do!), I will be able to assure them this will pass. Peace will descend once again. I have the perspective of time, you see, and that gives me all the foundation I need to have hope for the future.

Of course, the purpose of the Fill is not to provide a sanctuary for people seeking peace. Its purpose is not even to provide a sanctuary for birds. The site is owned by the University of Washington, and its main purpose is education. This makes me uneasy. I've been an educator myself for 20 years, and I know how quickly public education can abandon one program for another. At the moment, the Union Bay Natural Area (the place birders call Montlake Fill) is an educational laboratory for environmental students. Not everyone at the university agrees with this purpose, however. In the past, the Athletics Department thought a better educational purpose for this place would have been to provide a couple of soccer fields, or maybe a nine-hole golf course.

Even if the College of the Environment continues to manage UBNA under the aegis of the UW Botanic Gardens, as it does now, I worry that this unique place will not be safe. For years, people have been calling on our public institutions to think and act more like businesses. Successful businesses make money. They don't depend on government tax dollars to stay afloat—unless, that is, they are giant agribusinesses, multinational petroleum companies, big banks, or major car manufacturers. (Don't get me started.)

Because of this kind of thinking, the university has received less and less support from the state legislature. To make up the difference, the UW's departments are expected to raise more money from outside sources. I guess, ideally, the goal is for each department to become profitable.

For departments such as UW Botanic Gardens, the possibilities for "adjusting their revenue streams," as the new president, Michael K. Young, delicately puts it, are limited. Plant sales, facilities rentals, a little gift shop, and the sale of parking spaces on fields during events all bring in a few dollars. Stepping up grant applications might bring in more, although the grant-giving world has shrunk in this recession. Reducing labor costs is a business-tested way to improve profitability, and indeed, the UW's part-time gardener has been let go. And still the cuts keep coming, the demand for a blacker bottom line.

Author Philip Pullman encountered the same kind of thinking in his own community of Oxford, when the county council proposed to cut 20 of the county's 43 public libraries. In his testimony against the proposed cuts, Pullman said there are things we treasure in life that are completely outside the concept of economic value. One of them, for him, was the library. "Market fundamentalism, this madness that's infected the human race," he said, "is like a greedy ghost that haunts the boardrooms and council chambers and committee rooms from which the world is run these days.... The greedy ghost understands profit all right. But that's all he understands. What he doesn't understand is enterprises that don't make a profit, because they're not set up to do that but to do something different....

"I love the public library service for what it did for me as a child and as a student and as an adult. I love it because its presence in a town or a city reminds us that there are things above profit, things that profit knows nothing about, things that have the power to baffle the greedy ghost of market fundamentalism, things that stand for civic decency and public respect for imagination and knowledge and the value of simple delight."

Philip Pullman was well aware it takes money to keep libraries open, just as I am aware it takes money to maintain the Fill. It takes money to educate our children and preserve our environment, too. But money is not why we have children or love nature. We do not expect a return on investment from the things we cherish.

If you were to ask even the most sharp-penciled economist what is most important in life, you would hear answers such as "my family," "my profession," "my happiness." What we care most about has no monetary value at all. Love. Fulfillment. Joy. Our children. The beauty of nature.

Our deepest values are not economic. They have nothing to do with the market. But they are the things that make life worth living. The Fill is one such thing. Even a duck as dim as my favorite Cinnamon Teal knows that. Value is not the same as money.

21. Gotta Dance, Gotta Sing

One of the sounds I love best in summer is the song of the House Finches. House Finches are the quintessential example of what we birders call LBBs (little brown birds). The females and juveniles are a nondescript combo of muted brown and beige that allows them to simply vanish from view whenever they hop onto an equally brown and beige branch. The males have a little red here and there, but somehow it all blends into the browns and disappears from notice.

I've sat in front of blackberry bushes knowing a House Finch was mere feet from my face, and yet I couldn't pick it out from the foliage. Other times, I've seen one or two in a bush, and then, when they get startled by something, a bazillion fly out, like clowns exiting the Clown Car at a circus. They were obviously perching in plain sight all the time, but their nondescriptness hid them like magic.

What the House Finches lack in appearance, though, they make up for in song. House Finches have one of the most complex, beautiful songs in all of bird-dom. In spring, the males give concerts that go on and on, never seeming to repeat themselves. Not tuneful, exactly, since I can never quite identify a pattern; more like an improvised operatic run, when the tenor takes one note from the score and won't let go of the spotlight for long minutes at a time.

Now that it's summer, the males have mostly stopped singing. Instead, they and their families are tootling. It's a musical conversation they carry on with each other, and it is lovely. I guess they just can't help singing, even when they're only passing idle comments.

Another bird who can't seem to stop singing throughout the summer is the little Willow Flycatcher male who set up shop in

Willow Flycatcher © Thomas Sanders

the dead willow snag on Main Pond this year. Willow Flycatchers belong to the Empidonax family. There are eleven different species of Empidonax that come to the U.S. from Central and South America to breed every summer. The distinguishing characteristic of Empidonax flycatchers is that there is no distinguishing characteristic. They all look alike: brownish to olive backs, grayish to yellowish fronts, a couple of whitish wingbars, whiskers around the beak. Not a peacocky family. In fact, they're all LBBs (or, if you're from Texas, LBJs—little brown jobs). Oh, you can see minor differences in eye-rings, yellow wash on the belly, bill length and color, tail length, and such. But the truth is, the best way to tell one flycatcher from another is to hear its song.

That's what I love so much about my little Willow Flycatcher: his song. Every morning, he flies up to the topmost branch of the snag and waits while the House Finches amassed there tootle their complex melodies. The finch confab goes on and on while the Willow waits in the wings, so to speak. Finally, the finches leave, and the flycatcher takes his place on the topmost branch of the snag. He swells himself up like Pavarotti. His little neck bulges, his beak points itself up to the heavens, and forth pours the singer's aria: "FITZ-bew! FITZ-bew! FITZ-bew!"

I have to say the Willow's song is down at the far end of the bell curve of euphony. Many people would scarcely classify it as song at all. It's only two rough notes, sung over and over. More the crankcase than the heavenly trump. But to the singer, his music is sublime. You can see he thinks so because of the way he looks around for a listening female after he finishes one particularly energetic burst. He obviously believes his talent is great enough to bowl over any gal in the vicinity.

It's a lesson for all us seemingly untalented talents. To an outsider's ear, our song may not qualify us to appear on stage, but it is uniquely ours. No one else can sing it as we do. No one else ever has or ever will. Therefore, sing it loud and sing it proud. Your song is beautiful. It will bring happiness to all those who care about you, just as the Willow Flycatcher's song brings a smile to all who hear it.

It is as beautiful in its way as the song of the House Finch, who sings great but looks dowdy. Listening to the chorus of finch music at the Main Pond, I am reminded that outward appearance is just as unimportant in life as raw talent. The thing that really matters is what you do with your gifts, whether they are small or large.

Anita Kuroiwa knows this well. She is a former ballerina, now dance teacher at Seattle Academy. From the age of four, she knew she wanted to be a classical dancer, but in those days, black ballerinas were shunned by the dance world. Kuroiwa recalls going to New York auditions and asking the dance captain, "How many are you taking?" She meant, how many black dancers.

"People would be very honest," she says. "'We're taking one girl; we're taking one boy.' They might have been looking for 50 dancers, but they were taking one black female and one black male."

Kuroiwa also recalls other forms of discrimination, including body form. "The rationale of the producers is that the audience pays to see a certain image when they walk in the door, so consequently producers are paying the dancers to provide that image. It's the job. If you do not provide that image, then goodbye."

When she was twelve, Kuroiwa left the safety of her neighborhood dance school and entered the general population. She was the only black dancer in ballet class, and the instructor was not happy to see her. She asked Kuroiwa why she wasn't in tap class with the other blacks, only she used a far less polite word. Kuroiwa made up her mind then and there that she would do something to change the world. "Someday," she told herself, "I'm going to create a place where dancers can feel free to dance without all the malice of discrimination."

At Seattle Academy, she founded Dansation, a professional-style school of dance for any student who has the desire and drive to learn this art form. Kuroiwa doesn't care what students look like or how much inborn talent they have. "The best part of being a dance teacher is sharing the knowledge," she says. "My job is important because I think I can make a difference in somebody's life. I honestly think that is the universal human wish for immortality. One way to do that is to keep passing on what we know to other people. That's what I do for my dance students. There was a lot of discrimination when I was a dancer. 'You're too fat.' 'You're too tall.' 'You're too thin.' 'You're too whatever.' I wanted to create a vehicle for young people to be able to study without all of that ugliness, where they could really learn to love the art of dance, as I do. I've been dancing for over half a century now. I'm still in love with the dance. I guess I always will be."

Kuroiwa passes along to her students as much of her dance knowledge as she can. But perhaps the best lesson she teaches them is: When you love something, don't let anyone or anything stop you from doing it. Like my favorite flycatcher, if you've got to sing, just let 'er rip.

Ladies-tresses' Orchids © Doug Parrott

22. Kindness

Some years ago, I attended a parade at the Marine Corps Barracks in Washington, D.C. The Marines were honoring those wounded in Iraq and Afghanistan by dedicating one of their weekly parades to them. Prior to the parade, there was a reception in a big tent pitched near the commandant's house. As I wandered around in the tent, vainly trying to find something nonalcoholic to drink, I came upon a poster mounted on an easel. It said, "We are at war. Are you doing all you can?"

I've been thinking about that question ever since. Whether people agree with the war or whether they oppose it, our young men and women are overseas fighting it. They are doing so at our behest. Are we doing all we can to help them?

Or to put it a more direct way, is there anything that I—an aging woman with little money and bad knees—can do to help?

Well, sure, there is plenty I can do. More than anything, I can foster kindness. It may sound loopy, but I have come to believe that if each one of us grows strong enough and big-hearted enough to show kindness and generosity to others, then eventually there will be no more war. Kindness leads to empathy, empathy to understanding, understanding to tolerance. You can't fight someone whom you understand and whose humanity you feel you share.

So lately I've tried my best to always be kind. It's a drop in the big bucket of human endeavor, to be sure, but it's a start. Maybe kindness will spread, like that cup of coffee someone bought for the driver behind him at a drive-up coffee shop in Missouri. Next thing you know, everyone was buying a cup of coffee for the guy behind him. Maybe people realized you have to start kindness somewhere, or you risk falling into despair.

My beliefs were put to a severe test today, though. I was creeping over the wooden bridge across University Slough, sneaking up on the Virginia Rail that is supposed to strut up and down the road here like a runway model showing off her latest Versace. Normally, Virginia Rails are shy, secretive birds who hate being stared at. This one seemed to be the extroverted exception, so my hopes were high that I would see it. Suddenly a loud voice blew my hair straight back and stimulated me to set a new record for the standing broad jump. "What are you seeing?" bellowed a woman who had popped out of nowhere. "I'm a birder too!!"

My first impulse was to raise both hands in the air and run around in circles, ululating the loudest primal scream ever. I have been trying to see this rail every morning for weeks. I've gotten out the door by 6 a.m., forgoing my second cup of coffee, still bleary-eyed, while my husband sits by the heater and chirps, "Better luck this time." I was sure this morning I would hit the jackpot, but now, thanks to Mrs. Megaphone, all the rails in every ditch and pond on the entire site had no doubt retired for the day.

My hands twitched toward her, but then I remembered that I'm supposed to be fostering kindness. Swallowing the words that were burbling upwards like Mount Etna about to let go, I calmly answered, "There's a mother Wood Duck with nine babies in the slough." No use mentioning the rail that would have to take tranquilizers before it ever came out again.

The woman's face lit up. "Oh," she said, "I was here once when the baby Barn Swallows had just fledged. They were perched in a row on the railing and looked so cute." She went on to tell me that her daughter was playing a volleyball match, and she was on her way to watch. I wished her well, and we parted.

I can't say my frame of mind was happy. I mean, I had lost any chance of seeing that pesky Virginia Rail. I didn't much care about baby Barn Swallows perched on a railing in somebody else's past

Juvenile Red-necked Phalarope © Kathrine Lloyd

lifetime. On the other hand, I had kept my resolution to be kind. There's got to be a reward in that, doesn't there?

There was. Or maybe it was just the Fill being the Fill. Not 15 minutes later, a black and white streak flashed by and materialized on top of the greenhouse at the Youth Garden: an Eastern Kingbird, flown in from who knows where and who knows why. Eastern Kingbirds are supposed to confine themselves to east of the Cascades, but here it was, black shoe-button eyes gleaming in the sun, white-banded tail flipping gently up and down. The bird posed for some ten minutes or maybe an hour—I was too lost in time to tell.

I have had many moments like this at the Fill. There was the time, for example, when I saw two Spotted Sandpipers bobbing their clownish rear ends as they probed the mud of Main Pond with their long bills. Spotted Sandpipers are one of my favorite birds, especially during breeding season, when they acquire big black polka dots on their bellies. These two were in the middle of changing their feathers to the more sedate plain brown and white of their winter dress, when they become so nondescript it is hard to identify them at all. I figured this was a good chance to bone up on my field marks.

As the two worked their way north and disappeared into the willows along the shore, a movement nearby caught my eye. A juvenile Red-necked Phalarope was swimming in the water, its little feet paddling to stir up crustaceans and bring them to the surface, where it could pick them off with its needle-sharp beak. Its soft black eyes were lined with black, like King Tut wearing kohl. A tiny drop of water dangled from its bill, glistening diamond-bright. The bird stopped swimming and glanced up at me. For an instant, our eyes met—two alien creatures, making a connection, however brief, however far from each other's lives. Oh, oh.

Einstein said that as we approach the speed of light, time slows down. I don't know any physics, but I do know that when the light shines on a rarely beautiful bird like this one, time does stop.

How I wish everyone in the world could have shared that one moment with me. No hate. No war. Just the peace that dwells in our hearts when joy fills us up.

23. Never-Ending Story

Two birders stood at the north end of Shoveler's Pond, gazing south over the rolling hills to the cattails on the shore and to the blue water of Lake Washington beyond. In the distance, Mount Rainier gleamed pink and gold in the early morning sunlight, like some poet's dream of heaven.

The foreground, however, was not as celestial. Fire had come to the Fill the night before, and now the fields lay seared, black and bare. The lone Ponderosa Pine that had for years stood guard at the top of the hill was burned from crown to base. The plastic tubes protecting the newly planted Garry Oak saplings had melted. Here and there, a bare stalk of chicory stuck up, but all else was gone, leaving only white ash and black soot behind.

"What a difference a day makes," said one birder, shaking his head. We both remembered the waving fields of prairie grass, bending their graceful heads in the breeze, the blue bonnets of chicory flowers flung widely onto the golden carpet, the yellow of Hairy Cat's-ear dotting the scene. Now gone, thanks to the colossal stupidity of the Firecracker Boys, a gaggle of local teenagers who somehow thought it would be a good idea to set off fireworks in a bone-dry field of combustible grasses.

And yet, I can't say yesterday's scene made me sad, for it was not entirely a picture of loss. Fire and prairie are long-time companions (though not, perhaps, in the heart of a big city). Fire rids the prairie of unwanted weeds, fertilizes the soil with ash, burns the seeds in a way that attracts many birds. Indeed, the American Goldfinches,

Mourning Dove in burnt Lone Pine Tree © Thomas Sanders

House Finches, Savannah Sparrows, and Common Yellowthroats who live here were already gathered in large flocks, foraging for the bounty the fire had given.

Change comes constantly to the Fill, sometimes fast, as with this fire; more often slowly over many years. The Fill as we know it today is the result of Lake Washington being lowered nine feet when the Ship Canal opened. The boggy land that emerged when the lake retreated became a landfill in 1926. Five decades later, when the landfill closed, the University of Washington set aside much of it as Union Bay Natural Area (UBNA), one of the premier birding sites in the state.

Long before humans put their stamp on it, though, change was the order of the day for this little patch of nature. Lake Washington, after all, has come and gone many times in the geologic past, as ice ages saw sheets of glaciers inch down from the north, scour the Puget Sound Basin, retreat, and then repeat. Fourteen thousand years ago, the hill where the birder and I stood was buried under 3,000 feet of solid ice. Eleven thousand years ago, the ice was gone, and the birds were back.

I began birding here in the 1980s. In those days, prairie and ponds dominated the landscape. Now there is much more riparian habitat. The birds who use the Fill reflect these changes. When the Fill was mostly marsh and dump, shorebirds and gulls dominated. Now we get a more diverse mixture: fewer shorebirds and gulls and a lot more songbirds. We're even starting to get forest birds such as Red-breasted Nuthatches.

To me, it's all beautiful because it's all part of wild nature. In a way, I hope it keeps changing forever. In another way, though, I hope it never changes.

Change is chancy, as any geneticist will tell you. Mutations can be good, but many are bad, even lethal. In fact, when organisms experience too rapid a rate of genetic change, they often create what biologists call error catastrophe. Error catastrophe is extinction.

Perhaps the sheer risk of the new going bad is why most of us dislike change. Things might not be perfect the way they are, but at least they're familiar. Better to dance with the devil you know, as the saying goes, than the devil you don't.

But do we dislike all change? That's hard to answer. When winter changes into spring, people are glad for warmer weather and more sunshine. When the Tree Swallows return to Seattle, birders rejoice. "Did you hear today that the Tree Swallows are back at Ridgefield?" one birder asked me this past spring. His face was lit up with the same inner joy that gardeners feel when the soil gets warm. Ridgefield is one of the southernmost national wildlife refuges in the state. When spring migrants show up here, we know it won't be long before we see them at the Fill.

That same birder looked most unhappy a few days later. "Did you see the wooden bench down at East Point?" he asked, outraged. "Why would anyone want to turn this wild place into a city park!!??"

He made one bench sound as heinously unnatural as the Fun Forest arcade at Seattle Center, but really it is a wooden memorial to a dearly departed person who loved nature. The bench is the UW Botanic Garden's latest attempt to raise money for a budget that has been repeatedly cut. The hope is that many people will want to memorialize their loved ones by donating money to the Center for Urban Horticulture. The current cost of a memorial bench is $8,000.

I suppose the outraged birder thought the bench was just the vanguard of hosts of wooden settees. In his imagination, benches would soon be marching down every trail at the Fill, as unstoppable and annoying as the multitudinous brooms that Mickey Mouse conjured into being when he was the Sorcerer's Apprentice. Along with the benches would come civilized picnics, people sunning themselves on beach towels, boom boxes belting out the latest teen music, and the smell of roasted hot dogs clogging the air currents as surely as wieners clog arteries.

Jared Diamond might say my friend was outraged because he was used to the way the Fill looked now and did not want the future Fill to look any different. Diamond, in his book *Collapse,* speculated about how people react to environmental change. One of his study areas was Easter Island.

Easter Island, in the South Pacific, is one of the most isolated islands in the world. The nearest major land mass is Chile, more than 2,000 miles away. Before Polynesian settlers arrived sometime between 300 and 1200 A.D., Easter Island was a pristine, heavily forested wilderness, with at least 22 species of trees, five species of land birds, and 25 species of breeding seabirds. After the arrival of man, the ecology of the island rapidly deteriorated. First to go were the land birds, all of which became extinct, followed eventually by the huge trees that the islanders used for building sea-going canoes. The canoes were needed to enable the islanders to catch dolphins, their most reliable food source. The extinction of the large trees was followed by the extinction of every single tree species on the island: total deforestation. This was followed by massive extinctions of seabirds—all but nine species lost—as the people consumed their own ecology.

The collapse of the island's ecology led to the collapse of the island's civilization as well. A rich, thriving culture of 15,000 people ended up hanging on by a thread. When Europeans arrived in 1722, they found an estimated 3,000 people.

One day, as Diamond and his students discussed the disaster, a student raised his hand and asked, "What did the man who cut down the last palm tree say?"

Diamond realized this was a most profound question. Indeed, what would a person think who pounded in the final nail of an entire culture's coffin?

Upon reflection, Diamond concluded the man wouldn't think anything at all. You see, to that man, Easter Island was already virtually treeless. Maybe there were still a couple of little saplings growing here and there, but for the most part, the land had already turned into a poorly maintained steppe. The man had no notion it used to be any different. The transformation from edenic forest to hellish wasteland had happened gradually, over many generations. There was no meaningful record of the past, no way for current residents to imagine it. Even when the memory of giant trees was still alive, people could look around and see saplings growing. They must have thought the big trees would always grow back. They didn't know about soil science, botany, or demographics.

To that mythical man with an ax, the way Easter Island looked to him was the way it had always looked. More than that, it looked the way it was *supposed* to look.

Diamond calls this phenomenon "landscape amnesia." He means that when ecology changes gradually, people accept the changes without even noticing them. That's partly because the larger change is lost in the "noise" of minor fluctuations that occur from day to day, even from year to year. But it's also because the slowness of change gives people a chance to get used to new circumstances gradually enough so everything still seems normal. Diamond calls this "creeping normalcy."

It's important to point out there is still plenty of nature on Easter Island. It just isn't the same nature that was there 2,000 years ago. It's a poorer nature, less diverse, less able to support human life. But it's also robust in its own way. People can't really destroy nature. Life is too strong for that. In time, new species will arise to take advantage of the specific conditions that now exist on Easter Island, and for that matter, anywhere else on the planet.

The real question, then, for environmentalists, isn't: How do we save nature? Nature is quite good at saving itself. A better question is: How do we save the nature that exists today? Or, more pertinent: How much are we willing to sacrifice to preserve the species we have right now?

For, to preserve nature in its current form, we cannot think about saving a photogenic species here and there. Saving one species is relatively easy. Polar bears, for example, can be raised quite successfully in zoos. But to preserve all that a polar bear *is* means preserving its entire ecology. To do that, we will have to address global climate change, resource sustainability, population growth, and worldwide standards of living. Are we up to making the hard choices in our lives that would preserve enough ecology to enable species to survive? Can our governments cooperate in ways we have never before imagined? Can we live, in short, within our ecological means?

Green Heron © Thomas Sanders

When I look at the bench that so offended my friend, I see great hope for the future. I remember when the workers arrived to install the bench. I came upon them digging a foundation underneath the tall cottonwoods that overhang Waterlily Cove. "Whatcha doing?" I asked, sauntering up.

"We're putting in a memorial bench," answered one worker.

"Wow," I said, "that's great, but don't you think this is a dangerous place for a bench? I mean, cottonwood trees are known to drop their limbs without warning. Maybe you guys should move the bench to a safer spot, like the gardens around the CUH building." Far from the wilds of the Fill, in other words.

My concern might have touched off a bit of a firestorm, as UW administrators tried to figure out whether putting a bench under a dangerous tree was wise. An arborist came out and said yes, indeed, cottonwood limbs could fall without warning. But the family liked the location. The view of marsh, lake, and Mount Rainier was unsurpassed. The bench went in as planned.

I never sit on the bench. In fact, I rarely tarry at all on that portion of the trail. I see too many big limbs lying around on the ground, and my imagination is too vivid.

Nevertheless, I respect the family that insisted on putting the bench there. Their decision flew against science. It even defied fear of litigation. It was an act made out of pure love of nature.

Something about the strength of that act warms my heart. Nutty? Perhaps, at least to my mind. But love is often nutty, seldom logical.

For love, we will disregard common sense. Out of love, we will change our behavior. We will make sacrifices that do not even feel like sacrifices. Love always has been and always will be the best hope of the world. When it comes to love of nature, we can use all of it we can get.

Let us therefore try to love nature enough to change ourselves and alter our impact on the land. For love, let us preserve all the species that share the planet with us. Starting right now.

24. Stop

I think of nature as slow-moving. One season gradually fades into another as the Earth in its orbit tilts us first toward the sun and then away from it. Our world takes an entire year to go around once, then repeats the transit, over and over again. And so the years pass into decades, the decades into centuries, and the eons flow by, a slow-moving river of time without end.

Out at the Fill, as the days slip by uncounted, I observe the wild things as they keep doing what they have done for thousands of years. The trees add a ring to an already thick trunk. The cattails grow their brown flower spikes in the late summer, preparing to give their fluff to the chickadees for nests in the coming spring, year after everlasting year.

Meanwhile, we humans scurry from one appointment to another, our days filled with too long to-do lists, burdened with more items to check off than anyone could possibly do in a day. Cars filled with frantic commuters crowd the floating bridge's lanes from dawn to dusk and beyond, as we rush to work, hurry home to make dinner, cram in a quick jog or a fast gulp of latte. If only the sun would slow its long slog across the sky just a wee bit more and give us a 25-hour day, think what we could stuff into that extra hour.

In reality, though, it is nature that rockets through time, not we. To see this is true, all you have to do is study the Bewick's Wren family that popped into view at the Wedding Rock today. The two babies have fledged enough feathers to enable them to flap after their parents, begging incessantly for food. They were at it this morning in

Juvenile Bewick's Wren © Doug Parrott

a bush just two feet from my camp stool. The dad was rushing from branch to branch, trying desperately to catch enough bugs to shut them up. (I say the dad not because I'm sure of his gender—with Bewick's Wrens, it's hard to tell—but because he was willing to truck back and forth from the relatively buggy Alder Grove to the bush near me where the babies were crying. A female, I feel sure, would have insisted on the babies coming at least as far as the table. But all the dad could do was mutter, "I'm coming, I'm coming," as he fetched one bug after another.)

He and his mate have been caring for the babies for several weeks now, which sounds long but is nothing compared to the amount of time John and I have been caring for our kids. The Bewick's Wrens (like all birds) mate, lay, brood, hatch, and raise their young all in one short season. They accomplish in four months what it takes humans to do in four times four years—minimum. Young wrens are teenagers for what? Two weeks? Three, tops. Mine took eleven years to get through their teens, and that's not counting their present years as twenty-somethings, when they still come home to roost occasionally and ask for a bug.

Wild nature is a searing bolt of lightning compared to the slow-cooker of human nurture. And because our lifespan is long compared to a wren's, maybe we should carve out some of it just to savor slowly on one of these lazy, hazy days of summer. We do have the time to slow down.

Of course, nobody in our society really believes this. We tell ourselves we should stop and smell the roses, but that mantra is a lot like the one we say when we try to lose 10 pounds before summer so we can fit into our bathing suits better. Like that's gonna happen.

On the other hand, before you can make a change in your habits, you have to make a commitment. For one of my New Year's resolutions this year, I decided I would try to make people stop, if just for a moment, to savor life. I made this commitment partly to answer the question, "While Messiah tarries, what should one do?"

The question came up when I got my husband a book of Maimonides's writings. Maimonides was a medieval Jewish scholar whose works are still revered and consulted today. One of Maimonides's most famous sayings has to do with the coming of the Messiah: "I believe with a full heart in the coming of the Messiah, and even though he may tarry, I will wait for him on any day that he may come."

Jewish tradition is filled with folk wisdom about the coming of the Messiah (including Woody Allen's take on how, when the Messiah establishes his kingdom, the wolf will lie down with the lamb, "but," suspects Allen, "the lamb won't get any sleep").

Devout people believe in the coming of the Messiah—or his second coming, if you're Christian—but they are philosophical about his timing. In Russian Jewish tradition, there is a joke about this. A man sees his friend standing at the edge of the village and asks him what he is doing. "I've got a job. When Messiah comes, I'm supposed to be the first one to greet him," the man answers.

"How much are you getting paid?" asks his friend.

"One ruble a month."

"That isn't very much," the friend points out.

"No," admits the man, "but the job is permanent."

Given that the wait has been long and may well be a lot longer still, what should we do while we're waiting? Or, to put it in more secular terms, if paradise is not coming around the bend—if the perfect mate or the perfect job or the perfect life has not dropped from the heavens at our feet—how should we spend our time?

We could spend it just waiting for something good to happen. Many people do. We could spend it helping to make the world better, knowing we won't achieve perfection but adding our mite anyway. Many people do that, too. We could be selfish or selfless, cruel or kind, hopeful or in despair.

Aki Kurose, one of the many people in my life who have taught me how to live well, decided she would spend her time on Earth working for peace and racial tolerance. She was a Quaker who, at age 15, had been transported to the internment camp at Minidoka during World War II because she was Japanese American. She never got over the injustice of that act, nor her abhorrence of the war that had prompted it.

When the war ended and Kurose returned to Seattle, she began putting her ideals into practice. She became a first-grade teacher and taught her students to seek peace. She made her home into a center where people of all races could meet to oppose racism. She encouraged Asian Americans to enter politics. Gary Locke, the first Asian American governor in the continental U.S., credited her for starting his political career. Aki worked for open housing, equal opportunity for all, early childhood education, and respect for children. To her, these were all aspects of peace. Before she began class each day, she would take her students outdoors and tell them to send their sadness, hurt, and anger upward and away, into the atmosphere. It was her way of teaching children to seek inner peace. She used to say, "Without peace, real learning cannot take place. Real interaction with others...meaningful interaction, cannot take place."

Aki died after a 17-year struggle against cancer. She has been much honored since then, with a school named after her, a housing development named after her, a peace garden made in her name, even a day set aside to honor her.

I'm sure Aki would have been grateful for all the honors, but I wonder sometimes if she would consider herself to have been as successful as the honors imply. World peace is still beyond our reach. Inner peace is still a dream for most of us. Aki dedicated her life to peace, and yet the world and the human heart are still filled with war. Since she did not achieve her goals, I ask myself: Were her efforts futile? Was Aki a failure?

In our results-driven, accountability culture, surely the answer would be yes, Aki failed dismally. But that is not the way Maimonides would assess her efforts, or her life. He would ask instead, as he would ask of us all: Did you spend your time here in worthwhile endeavor?

Not all of us have the pleasure of working at a job we love. Not all of us have the good health we would like so we can do the things we want. We rush through our days heedless of the beauty around us, too busy to be kind to the ones we love, too frazzled to take care of the things that really matter. It doesn't have to be this way.

One morning I arrived at the Fill just as a rain shower was moving off to the north, leaving the bushes and flowers at the start of Wahkiakum Lane glistening with diamond drops. The sun came out, and a perfect rainbow appeared over the Youth Garden. I stopped and stared, mouth open. I could see every color, from rich red at the top to soft violet at the bottom, each color more beautiful than the next. As I stood there, transfixed, people pushed past me on their way to work. I think many of them were late, they hurried so. "Look at that," I said to each one, but no one would stop. One man went racing past on his bicycle. "Do you see the rainbow?" I shouted to his retreating back. I thought he would just keep pedaling toward his deadline, as everyone else was. But he screeched to a halt, leaped off his bike, and came running back to join me. We watched until the rainbow faded into the blue of the far sky. Then we turned to smile at each other.

Time in its rush stopped, and we shared a moment, just a moment, of perfect tranquility. We were at peace.

Buttercup © Doug Parrott

Part IV
Fall

25. Free Spirit

Cliff Swallows enjoy doing everything together. Like a gaggle of eighth-grade girls, they travel together, eat together, roost together, and dress alike.

This year, Cliff Swallows arrived at the Fill from their homes in South America on April 4. One day, no swallows; the next, sky filled with them. They congregated mostly on the western side of the Fill, not too far from their colony of mud nests plastered under the eaves of the UW's IMA (Intramural Activities) Building. The nests have long been a thorn in the side of the Athletics Department. Athletes, coaches, and fans like to park under these eaves, and they all dislike bird decorations on their cars. When people make enough of a fuss, the department orders maintenance staff to scrape off the nests. The maintenance workers comply, despite the official-looking signs epoxied at intervals onto the walls of the building. The signs say, "These mud nests are made by CLIFF SWALLOWS and are protected by international law. Unauthorized disturbance will be prosecuted."

The signs look official, but it turns out they were installed by a Dr. Michael Beecher of the Psychology Department, a guy who just happens to like Cliff Swallows.

Luckily, nature is sometimes stronger than even college sports. The Cliff Swallows remember their ancestral colony and return to it year after year, whether the nests are still there or scraped off. Almost immediately after arrival, the swallows commence construction. This year was no exception. Soon after arriving from the south, the swallows flew over to the IMA to check out their nesting site.

Undeterred by human efforts to deny them a building permit, the Cliff Swallows flew to Main Pond to collect mud to repair the old nests and create some new ones.

As they renovated the colony, the swallows took their lunch breaks together—of course—flying around the Lagoon, where insects breed abundantly in the still waters. Every morning during nesting season, I walked over to say hello. Cliff Swallows are early risers, like me, and the rising sun would find them already out and about.

Last week, though, the colony was deserted. Ah, I thought, moving day. Like most birds, Cliff Swallows can hardly wait to leave behind their nests. Nests are not birds' homes. On the contrary, nests can be dangerous because they attract predators, so as soon as the nestlings can fly, everyone leaves.

Sure enough, the colony had moved itself to a little tree growing in the center of Canoe Island. Parents and kids were now all clutching branches there, waiting for the insects to warm up and begin flying. I counted more than 200 birds packed onto a tree not much bigger than an SUV. Everyone was chattering at once. Cliff Swallows are small birds with small voices, so I was surprised at the decibels they generated when in chorus. From a distance, they sounded like a flock of blackbirds. In fact, I thought the noise was the raucous Red-winged Blackbirds, who also hang out on Canoe Island. After I realized the cacophony was caused by the Cliff Swallows, I tried to analyze how many swallows it takes to duplicate the raucousity of a blackbird. Scientists will be pleased to know the ratio is 14:1.

For the next several days, the Cliff Swallows will continue to hunt insects together, building up strength and fat for the long journey south. Last year at this time, the flock decided to patronize Main Pond. I think the protected waters of the pond attracted them. Swallows drink on the wing, so it's helpful to find waveless water. To take a drink, they skim over the water, flying closer and closer to the surface. Then all at once, they raise their wings straight up, put their heads down, and take a tiny sip on the fly. It takes a lot of skill to drink on the wing like this—the juveniles tend to misjudge at first and make a mighty splash instead of a delicate ripple.

In early fall, you should keep an eye out to see this lovely phenomenon of nature, because it won't keep happening for long. One
night soon, the swallows will sense conditions are right. They will
rise into the night sky together, circle their summer home a time or
two, and wing their way south.

In the meantime, though, the flock goes about its business making
preparations for the journey. They are as diligent at this work as they
were at building their nests earlier in the year. Cliff Swallows always
strike me as the blue-collar members of the swallow clan, if swallows
wore collars. What I mean is, they are a hard-working, beak-to-the-
grindstone kind of bird. Life isn't easy for them. Thinking back to
the spring when they began nest construction, I recall watching them
gather mud by the tiny beakful, mix it to proper consistency, and
carry it back to the IMA. It took hundreds of beakfuls of mud to
make a nest, and dozens of swallows to make the colony.

Seeing them toil at the mud bank of the Main Pond, like Israelites
making bricks for Pharaoh, or watching them wing back and forth
endlessly now in fall, making fat for their trip, I have always assumed
that Cliff Swallows do not believe in partying till you drop. So it was
with jaw-dropping wonder that I watched a first-year Cliff Swallow
break off from his laboring brethren, float up into the ether, and
commence executing barrel rolls that would have put the Red Baron
to shame. With a casual dip of one wing, he tossed off a roll, flapped
a little to gain air speed, tossed off another roll, squeaked to the chain
gang below, and then did it all again.

There is a time of life when you feel so strong and vital that
exuberance fills every cell, and you simply must run, or dance, or do
a barrel roll.

Has that vitality passed from us baby boomers? Absolutely not!
We may have reached the age when we can't get up or down without
making a noise. We may think twice before bending over to pick
up something, and then when we're down there think about what
else we can do before we straighten up again. But inside, we are still
eighteen. And inside is where it counts.

Cliff Swallow making a nest © Tim Kuhn

26. Rights and Wrongs

The autumn winds tore through the Fill yesterday, sending all sensible creatures into cover. Birds, like other pilots, are reluctant to fly in strong wind because they know how dangerous a sudden gust or shear can be.

I, of course, was out here anyway. We Sidleses are not overly gifted with common sense. We don't let minor details such as the laws of nature dictate to us. Rather, we are free-range chickens, and my range is the Fill. I come here in all weathers, and I love the wind. It reminds me I am free, unless I have deadlines to meet, chores to do, and taxes to pay. Sigh, oh gusty sigh.

The juvenile Cooper's Hawks were out today, too. Unlike me, they're not chickens of any sort, but neither are they sensible. In fact, they are downright goofy, which is probably why I feel I have so much in common with them.

Earlier in the year, their parents dumped them off at the Fill to fend for themselves, and they've been learning how to hunt ever since. The other birds don't seem to take them very seriously. The American Goldfinch flock that has been feeding on chicory for the past several weeks perches in the same trees as the hawks do, and they chirp at their predators. Prey are not supposed to chirp. They are supposed to flee before the fierce attack of the mighty raptors, but the goldfinches just sit there. I guess Cooper's Hawks aren't born with fierceness; they have to build it, one small glare at a time.

All three juveniles were trying to catch food for the day, but since nobody else was out and about, they weren't having much luck.

They did drive away a Greater Yellowlegs, who had hunkered down on Main Pond to forage in the mud while the storm raged above.

The shorebird didn't want to leave its dinner table, but the hawks were just a little too present. So it finally jumped into the sky and flapped its way south, leaving the hungry hawks empty-clawed.

I was glad the yellowlegs got away this time, but I realize that the hawks have to eat, too. As a squall of rain blew in, I turned up my collar and headed for the car. I can go home to a pizza in the oven, but the birds must catch their own prey. They must find their own shelter against the elements and provide their own warmth, too. The penalty for failure is death.

That is why I find myself saying something to the people who come to the Fill and make the birds' lives harder than they already are: the dog walkers who let their dogs run off-leash; the people who trample new social trails in the fields and cattails; the litterers; the ROTC platoons who think the Fill is an ideal training ground for skirmish practice; the boys who carve donuts in the gravel by spinning out their muscle cars.

I have made enemies at the Fill. I don't want to, certainly don't like to. Sometimes when I push people by asking them to respect the wildlife, the people push back. Curses and anger are common responses, no matter how polite and respectful I try to be. There are times when I keep my mouth shut because I just don't have the energy to fly in the face of such disapproval. As the song says about John Adams in the musical *1776*, "You're obnoxious and disliked, that cannot be denied." Adams didn't often let the opinions of others stop him, but even he got discouraged by the unblinking stares of gimlet-eyed colleagues who tired of his admonitions and just wanted him to shut up.

On my low-energy days, I do shut up. But then I remind myself about the power of social pressure. I believe if we who love wildlife speak up and apply some social pressure, we will have a dramatic effect. Partly this is so because most people want to do the right thing. They haven't really thought about the negative impact one dog in a field can have on the birds trying to nest there. They are

Adult Cooper's Hawk © Dennis Paulson

unaware that littering their plastic packaging can poison birds who ingest it. They believe taking one walk through pristine cattails won't hurt the plants, not knowing that a cattail crushed is a cattail killed, not realizing that one set of tracks through a new field attracts more people to tramp there.

Applying social pressure is easy with people like this. Really, all a birder has to do is pick any bird who is adversely affected by humans and tell a story about that bird. I often pick Cooper's Hawks because they look so elegant but act so clumsy. As my husband says when he behaves in similar fashion, "My name is Bond. Clem Bond."

Sometimes, though, people do know the bad effects they have on nature, and they mistreat nature anyway. Take the Whatever Woman. She was a regular jogger around the Loop Trail, and she always ran with two dogs. One was on leash, the other not. I managed to stop her once long enough to explain how distressed the birds are by unleashed dogs. She listened for a few minutes and then said, "Whatever," continuing on her way with one dog on and one dog off.

The next time I encountered her, she wouldn't stop for a chat (or a scold). So I yelled as she went by, "Please put your dog on a leash."

"Whatever," she shouted back at me, and kept going.

Ocean Spray © Jean Colley

I told my birder friends about the Whatever Woman. "What can you do with a person like that?" asked one. "It's no use at all talking to her."

"On the contrary," I said, "we should make her our project. Every time we see her, we should each ask her to put her dog on a leash."

The idea of making Whatever Woman our project caught on. There was something about the idea of all of us working together toward a long-term goal that encouraged us to say something, even when we didn't want to. Soon, many birders were telling me about encountering her. They would ask her to put her dog on a leash, and every time they would get the same response.

One day, I was standing under the cottonwoods at Boy Scout Pond, chatting with two other birders. Far away in the distance, I heard a faint shout: "Whatever." Soon the Whatever Woman came running past. "Put your dog on a leash," we all shouted in unison. You can guess how she replied.

Ten minutes later, my friend and fellow birder Amy Davis hove into view. She saw I was laughing. "What's so funny?" she asked.

"I bet you told that jogger back there to put her dog on a leash," I said. Amy was astonished until I explained, "We could hear the Whatever Woman's response clear over here."

That was the last time I saw Whatever Woman. Maybe we wore her down, or maybe she decided she didn't want to encounter whole groups of birders telling her to change her habits.

I'm sorry we drove her away from the Fill but glad her dog isn't bothering the wildlife anymore. The Fill can absorb a truly astonishing amount of human impact and still provide good habitat for thousands of critters. But its capacity to absorb such pressures is finite. When the birds have so much to lose, and we have so little at stake, we owe it to nature—and to ourselves, for that matter—to limit our impact as much as we can. If that means giving up a small pleasure or enduring a slight inconvenience so a wild creature can have a better chance to survive, it is a sacrifice well worth making. Whenever.

27. Something Old, Something New

This past Saturday, I guided two Texas birders around my favorite place on Earth. They were here for a short visit and wanted to bird one of the most famous spots on the West Coast.

It's always fun to show newbies the Fill because you get to see the place anew through their eyes. Not that I need anyone to reopen my eyes to the glories of the Fill, mind you. I see wonders here every day. But I guess I've been at it long enough now so that I do sometimes overlook the gold right at my feet.

For example, *my* best bird on Saturday was a Solitary Sandpiper foraging on Shoveler's Pond. The Solitary was in migration, on its way from its breeding grounds in the muskeg of the Far North to its home in the tropics. Normally, Shoveler's Pond is as dry as a bone this time of year. But thanks to our cold, wet spring and non-summer, there was still some wet mud left in the pond's basin. The mud must have been loaded with insects and small crustaceans, because the bird was eating beakfuls of critters as fast as it could.

I don't get to see a Solitary Sandpiper every year, so this was a happy surprise. I was about to turn to my guests for a high-five, when I noticed they were looking at an entirely different bird: an American Goldfinch that had landed in the mud near the sandpiper.

American Goldfinches are so common at the Fill that I have ceased to notice them anymore. But the Texans were riveted. "Of course, we get goldfinches in Texas in the winter," they said, modestly declining to note that they get nearly every North American bird at some season or other in Texas. "But we never see them in their bright golden plumage."

Like many songbirds, male goldfinches molt in two main phases. In spring, they grow bright yellow feathers accessorized by black and white accents on their heads, tails, and wings. This getup is designed to appeal to the gentler sex. Once breeding season is over, the males shed their conspicuous feathers and grow drab winter dress, a kind of muddy, mustard brown-yellow with pale wingbars. But goldfinches follow their bliss when it comes to molting, and some of the males have declined to begin just yet. This particular male exhibited golden feathers that gleamed in the gray light of our Seattle fall like a small sun about to go nova.

"Ohhh," breathed the Texas birders, "how beautiful."

Yes, he truly was. And thanks to the vision of my new friends, I could see the glory of his beauty, too. Like the first goldfinch I ever saw. Like new.

I suppose it's a tired cliché to say we often fail to value what is most precious in our lives, if that precious thing is common or everyday. It's just too easy to take for granted. But oh how much we miss thereby.

I know this firsthand because I often do take the common birds at the Fill for granted, so much so that I don't really look at them beyond noting that yes, there is another finch or robin or chickadee. Whoop-de-doo. I like rarities so much more—the birds who show up maybe once in a lifetime. But because of my propensity to ignore the commonplace, I almost missed one of the rarest birds ever to appear at the Fill. It happened back in spring, on a very cold morning.

I was walking the Loop Trail near the Lone Pine Tree when what I thought was the bazillionth robin of the day flew out of the scrub around Main Pond and landed in a tree in Boy Scout Pond. I was supremely uninterested. For one thing, I was freezing, and the wind was howling, scaring up innumerable whitecaps on the lake. Not another soul was in sight—no doubt everyone else was probably

Male American Goldfinch © Tim Kuhn

sitting in front of a heater drinking coffee, I grumbled to myself. When the robin landed, I gave it a glance and kept walking. But then Dennis Paulson's voice rang in my mind.

Paulson is one of the state's foremost ornithologists and teaches Seattle Audubon's master birder classes. One day in class, he was asked for advice about how to be a better birder. He offered this chestnut: Look at every bird.

His advice was deceptively simple. *Of course* you're going to look at every bird, I muttered to myself on this day. Why else are you out here during the coldest, gloomiest spring Seattle has ever known? Why else did you get up before dawn and put on three layers of clothing, leaving your husband sitting beside the heater dressed in his PJs and drinking one steaming cup of coffee after another?

But Dennis knows what he is talking about. So often when we are out in nature, we think we are aware of what is all around us, but we don't stop and look. Thus, we don't really *see.* This is as oddly true of birders as it is for the joggers, dog walkers, and baby strollers who march through the Fill, rarely stopping to look at anything. Sure, we birders are there to look at birds, but we tend to see them as shapes, colors, and patterns of movement. If we see a flock of 200 Violet-green Swallows swirling over a field, we aren't going to look at every individual in the flock. We may stare at the flock for a while, trying to pick out a bird that flies differently or has a different shape or color, but if all the birds look about the same, we pass them by. The same is true if a lot of robins seem to be around. We'll look at the first couple, maybe, but after that we just say, "Oh, there's another robin." And we pass on.

I was about to do just that when Dennis spoke up, courtesy of the neurons he has permanently installed in my brain: Look at every bird. Sighing elaborately, I hoisted my binoculars up, and behold, there was a Loggerhead Shrike, its gorgeous gray and white feathers ruffled by the wind, its black mask standing out boldly, even in the dim light.

Loggerhead Shrikes are summer birds of eastern Washington. They fly up from the arid lands of Mexico and California to nest in the sagebrush of our deserts. They are songbirds, but also birds of prey, catching grasshoppers and other small animals with their hooked beaks. They are extremely rare at the Fill: only six have been seen here in the past 115 years. This one was preening unconcernedly in the cottonwood tree, but when it saw me looking, it flew away. I scurried after it, hoping to get another look.

The biting wind hit me with full force when I reached Hunn Meadow West, but I no longer cared, for on top of the little fruit tree in the field was the shrike, perched in full view. I stared, drinking in the beauty of this wild creature, who came with the storm and would not stay. It returned my stare for a moment, lifted its wings, and flitted north, gone as surely as the gray mist blown away by the wind. Only memory remained.

Meanwhile, as I was standing there, yearning after the shrike, another robin appeared. With heightened senses, I scanned it with my binoculars. Why, the robin was beautiful: flaming breast, black head, yellow bill, and bright eyes. I noticed the white stripes under its chin, matched by fluffy white patches near its tail. If robins were as rare as shrikes, our spirits would soar to the stratosphere upon seeing one. So why wait for the day when robin populations might become tiny? Better by far to take a moment to appreciate all the beauty in our lives while it is still here.

One year, my middle-school writing students worked on an oral history book about World War II. One of the veterans my kids interviewed was an Army officer whose job had been reconnaissance. He was a painter by trade, so his superiors figured he'd be good at noticing troop and gun placements forward of the Army's advance. His job was to infiltrate enemy-held territory until he found a spot where he could spy out where the German troops were positioned, how much firepower they had, and where the big guns were. Then he would radio the coordinates back to headquarters so our tanks and cannons could fire shells to destroy the enemy. It was very dangerous work because as soon as the Germans realized someone had spotted them, they would triangulate the radio signals and try to kill the spotter.

Male American Robin © Doug Parrott

Our interviewee had married his sweetheart just before he had left for the front. He missed her fiercely, so he wrote her a letter every day. In his pocket, he carried a cut-down paintbrush and a tiny set of watercolor paints, fitted into a tobacco tin. When he finished each letter, he sealed it in an envelope and then painted a little picture on the outside. Sometimes the paintings showed scenes where he was stationed. Other times the paintings were of his dreams. One of his wife's favorite paintings showed him lying on an Army cot in some godforsaken corner of war-torn Germany. He was fast asleep. Above his sleeping head, the painting showed the dream he was having; it was of her.

She saved every envelope and, all these years later, brought them in a large cardboard carton to show my students. As she pulled out one envelope after another, her face softened and grew younger. She smiled at one painting, then looked up into her husband's loving eyes. It was obvious to all of us that she and her husband were still as close as two people can be.

Their love was common, in the sense that they have felt it every day for more than 60 years, but it was far from ordinary. I do not believe a single day goes by when they take each other or their love for granted.

Neither should we take for granted the everyday people or things that we love. Abundance and familiarity do not lessen wonder. On the contrary, abundance gives us the chance to experience the sublime over and over again. Familiarity lets us deepen our understanding. We need only take the time to look and really see the treasure that lies all around our lives.

28. Ooh, Shiny

Seattle is about as far ecologically and psychologically from Oklahoma as one could imagine, but we do share at least one thing in common with our sister state. We both get terrific windstorms. Oklahoma has its Tornado Alley; Seattle has the Autumn Wind Tunnel.

Seattleites experience the Wind Tunnel whenever an especially intense low-pressure front develops at sea level in the northeastern Pacific Ocean, which it does occasionally in the fall. The front creates amazingly intense, sustained winds that blast toward us like a hurricane. "[We] don't call these storms hurricanes because they aren't tropical," says renowned Northwest meteorologist Cliff Mass, "but they pack a bigger punch. Huge size and big winds."

Such a storm arrived at the Fill on this November day, bending the cottonwood saplings almost double, blowing off the last of the autumn leaves, and giving the American Crows a big thrill. Unlike most birds—who seem to prefer hunkering down on a sturdy limb or under a dense bush to wait out the storm—crows seem to love the wild wind. They leap into the air like paragliders jumping off Mount Si, spread out their wings, and let their long black feather-fingers caress the air currents as the wind takes them where it will.

Five of them were at it over the greenhouse field this morning, when without warning, one of them broke formation and careened straight down. I thought it was going to crash into the greenhouse superstructure, like a World War II kamikaze exploding into an aircraft carrier, but no. The crow had simply been distracted by the silvery foil the CUH gardeners have strung up to keep the finches away from the plants. "Ooh, shiny."

170

I dislike crows on principle because of their seemingly gratuitous cruelty to other birds, but I must admit I greatly admire their ability to be distracted.

Not that lack of focus is usually considered a virtue. Certainly, I was not proud of the big fat "Unsatisfactory" on my elementary school report card under the subject of "Pays Attention." But even the threat of whole armies of U's marching down the columns of my report card could not make me stay attentive all day in a stuffy classroom. Life presented too many opportunities for me to be able to concentrate on just one thing. My teachers were not amused. They did everything in their power to instill the virtue of single-mindedness in all of us restless, squirming children.

Eventually, I guess they succeeded. In my adult life now—like most hard-driven people in our culture—I try to keep my eyes on the prize, nose to the grindstone, shoulder to the wheel. Productivity— that's the key. How else are you ever going to accomplish anything? Go anywhere? Make something of yourself?

But that crow who broke formation to investigate something shiny showed an exuberant ability not just to be distracted, but to live in the moment. And that is what I envy. Birds as a whole share this trait. Not for them the tensions of the modern world, the deadlines barreling down the track, the worries about the future, the baggage from the past. They exist in the here and now. In fact, I bet not a single one of them has ever needed a therapist to dig them out of an iffy past or guide them bravely into a scary future.

The Belted Kingfisher who stakes out the dead willow snags at the north end of Main Pond is another example of a live-for-the-moment bird. Belted Kingfishers are blue-gray bundles of energy with oversized beaks and a belligerent attitude. If they had shoulders, they would undoubtedly carry chips on them—disgruntled chips. Nothing in the world seems to make them happy. They're not quiet about their dyspeptic worldview, either. Kingfishers always seem to broadcast their disgruntlement in amplified voice no matter what else they're up to. Fly to a perch, time to complain. Sit on a branch, time to complain. Spot a rival, observe a birder, feel an itch—there's only one thing to do. Yiddish kvetchers like myself can only bow our heads in silent tribute.

But the fact is, kingfishers at the Fill have very little to complain about. They lead a pretty cushy life. For one thing, there are plenty of ponds and a big lake, all filled with fish for them to live on. Kingfishers get their food by diving for prey headfirst, stabbing a fish like D'Artagnon in a duel: *en garde, attaque, touché, et voilà: dejeuner.* At the Fill, *dejeuner* is easily come by.

I was watching my favorite female kingfisher execute her *attaque* one morning when all of a sudden, a young Cooper's Hawk burst out of hiding and rocketed toward her, talons at the ready to strike with killing force and turn the kingfisher into its own breakfast. The kingfisher leaped into the air and flapped for her very life. Being a kingfisher, though, she seemed constitutionally unable to refrain from complaining about this latest example of fate's inequity. So as she flew, she rattled off a string of invective that did nothing at all to slow her down. How she managed to execute her complicated twists and turns to throw off the hawk's pursuit while swearing so loudly, I'll never know.

Finally, in a masterful demonstration of aerobatic tactics, she performed some kind of a loop-the-loop too fast for the eye to follow and got behind the hawk, momentarily confusing the predator. Did she press her advantage and escape? No. Being a kingfisher, she let rage consume her and went on the attack herself, poking and prodding the hawk in midair until the poor thing gave up and fled.

The victorious kingfisher flew back to her perch in the willow snag, muttered a few more choice words, and then went back to fishing. Within moments, it was as if nothing had happened. An attack that would have prostrated me for days passed from her thoughts like flowing quicksilver. I always knew kingfishers had mercurial personalities, but this bird's ability to shake off the whole incident almost instantly was positively Zen-like. Talk about living in the moment.

So far from following her example, I tend to be more a disciple of Solon. Solon, you may recall, straightened out the Bronze Age

American Crow © Thomas Sanders

Athenians by giving them a new set of laws. Then he scurried off on a world tour so the Athenians wouldn't be able to get at him and make him alter any of the laws they disliked. In the course of his extended vacation, Solon stopped off to visit Croesus, the king of Lydia. Croesus was then—and still is—considered one of the richest men the world has ever known.

The king wanted the wisest man in the world to acknowledge the richest one, so he asked Solon to name the happiest man in all creation, expecting to hear that he filled the bill. All that wealth, you know. Instead, Solon named some obscure Greek guy who led a fulfilled life and died gloriously in battle.

Hmph, said Croesus to himself. All right, he thought, if I can't get top billing, at least I'll be second banana, so he asked Solon who was the second-happiest person in the world. Solon named two other obscure Greek guys, young men whose mother wanted to go to the town fête but had no transport, so her sons yoked themselves to her cart and dragged her on in. She was so proud of their filial feat that she asked the gods to reward her boys, which the gods promptly did by felling them on the spot. Everyone was totally satisfied—the boys died honored and happy, you see.

And that was Solon's point. He believed it's impossible to gauge your happiness level until the very end because, although it might look like you're happy now, who knows what awful fate lies around the next bend? Indeed, Croesus later lost all his wealth and became a slave wearing golden chains, which could not have been a happy experience for him. Solon's logic seems positively inescapable.

But let's think a bit about how that philosophy plays out day to day. For example, let's say you get a wonderfully restful night's sleep and wake to a morning bright with sunshine and birdsong. What a happy life you lead, you think smugly, as you stretch out on your satin sheets. Your husband hears you stirring and comes bustling in with a tray of coffee, orange juice, toast, and coddled eggs. "You deserve the best, my dear," he croons as he ladles on the jam. You smile fondly and wallow in this little fantasy of happiness— until you remember Solon and realize, yikes, a dark-matter asteroid undetectable by modern science might crash into the planet today. Even if you're lucky enough to escape the initial blast, you'll suffer a slow death when the Earth experiences the resulting nuclear winter. Your heart starts pounding. You're convinced you're about to have a coronary. The clouds move in, and there goes your sunny day. See, you weren't really happy at all, now were you?

In fact, the problem with Solon's philosophy is that you can never be happy today—you're too worried about what might happen down the road. And thus, Botox is born, as we all try to rid ourselves of the deep wrinkles we get from making frowny faces as we try to cope with unmanageable amounts of stress.

The scientists and philosophers among us think they have better ways to deal with the über-angst of modern life. Mathematicians tell us how to figure the odds. Dark-matter asteroids are extremely rare in our solar system. In fact, none has ever been detected, so the chances of one hitting us today are so remote as to be near zero. Psychiatrists advise us to imagine the worst-case scenario and realize we can handle it. The asteroid might hit, but we can always move down into the basement with our kids and live on canned peas, and how bad could that be? Theologians suggest we should leave it all to God. He knows what's going to happen anyway, and it's all part of His plan, so why worry?

And yet, worry creeps in. Like a gerbil running endlessly on its toy wheel, your mind spirals around and around uselessly. How can you stop it?

For me the answer is simple. I pick a windy day and go out to the Fill. I know it won't be long before I see something wonderful. It might be a crow diving on tinsel, or a kingfisher splashing up from the pond, shaking off glistening drops of water. Ooh, shiny. In those endless, timeless moments of indescribable beauty, I am distracted from the cares of the everyday world. My soul lifts, and I am transported to a place where joys will never end.

29. It's Ruddy Wet out There

Seattle, for the most part, luxuriates in mild weather throughout the year. Not for us the blizzards of wintertime Winnetka or the sweltering summers of St. Louis. Equinoctial storms that drench Midwest cities in downpours of violence are almost unknown here.

Our rain, by contrast, usually comes in a gentle drizzle that traces little wiggles on our windows, giving the child within us the opportunity to imagine silvery still-life paintings that never stay still for long.

Every now and then, though, when a cold front collides with the heat of an October afternoon, Seattle can get pummeled by thunderstorms so fierce they tear down 200-year-old trees. The trees cannot hold on when the wind and wet arm-wrestle them to the ground. The patriarchs simply lose their grip on the soil and fall.

So it was with growing alarm one hot day in October that I studied the sky over the Fill. Blue-black clouds were stacking up more than 20,000 feet high to the north. As I watched, they began to replace the clear blue of the sky with a kind of slate blue that looked vaguely cheerful until you realized all hell was going to break loose any minute.

I hurried down the Loop Trail past Main Pond, wondering whether I could get to my car more quickly by turning back or going forward. Unfortunately for me, quickness is not in my physical vocabulary anymore. It's not just because my knees don't work as well as they used to, and my fat layers have stocked my personal larder to outlast the Apocalypse. No, it's really because I cannot take more than 20 steps at the Fill without pausing to watch something interesting.

Male Ruddy Duck © Tim Kuhn

At East Point, the sun was still shining against the dark clouds, creating a special kind of light that bathed the Fill with glowing fire. The leaves drifting down from the cottonwoods looked lit from within. The air was so still I could hear the leaves patter as they struck the ground.

Swimming far out on the lake was a giant flotilla of ducks. They dotted the surface of the water as far as the eye could see, spread out like pumpernickel seeds on top of an acre-sized bagel. It was a gorgeous scene, and I decided the storm would just have to wait while I opened my camp stool and sat down to enjoy the calm.

The tableau did not last long. A Bald Eagle swooped in from the west, driving the ducks before it as it came. This particular eagle has dined on duck or coot every day for weeks, so the flock was wise to leap into the air quickly and fly around in a swirl too confusing for the eagle to single out anyone. Eventually, the eagle decided to quit trying and flew off.

Luckily for me, the flock settled down close to shore, and I was able to get a good look at all the members. Most were rather scruffy-looking Ring-necked Ducks in the middle of their molt, a sight I don't often get to see. Usually the Ring-necked males appear in public well preened and spiffy in their black-and-white suits, not a feather out of place. But these males had odd patches of brown mixed in with a little white and black here and there, as though they had just got out of bed, still sleepy-eyed and rumpled.

On the near side of the flotilla paddled a lone Ruddy Duck with big ideas about himself. He evidently thought he was in charge of the flock because he kept herding all the other ducks along. When a large Canvasback floated out of formation and crossed his path, the Ruddy hustled forward and clamped his bill onto the wing feathers of the Canvasback. I think the Ruddy was aiming for the Canvasback's neck, a common site for duck bites, but he just couldn't reach. The Ruddy was about half the size of the Canvasback, so I couldn't imagine the Canvasback would be much intimidated by this feeble attack, but I was wrong. Determination matters more than size, and the Canvasback hurried back into line without a murmur.

The runt-sized Ruddy Duck reminded me of a story my father told me about his training days in the Army during World War II. My dad belonged to an amphibious unit that was preparing to go to New Guinea. The training camp was led by a colonel so diminutive my father wondered how he had ever passed the physical to get into West Point. However, what the colonel lacked in size he made up for in feistiness. He took no guff from anybody.

One day a shipment of experimental life jackets arrived at the dock. Orders were to test them to see if they worked better than the bulky Mae West vests the men had been using. But the commanding officer, a young second lieutenant fresh out of officer training school, seemed paralyzed by the assignment. Should he order everyone to put on the new vests, or would one guinea pig do? Where was the nearest swimming pool? Could he commandeer it? What was the backup plan if the vests failed, and the men sank? Could any of them swim? As my dad's unit stood on the dock waiting for their commander to stop dithering and tell them what to do, the colonel appeared, a short stogie clamped in his jaws. "What's the holdup?" he growled.

The shavetail louie began to mumble an excuse about trying to devise the right experiment, but the colonel cut him off. "Give me that," he said, grabbing a life jacket and putting it on. Without another word, he strode to the end of the dock and kept walking right off into space. There was a splash, and then my dad saw the colonel in full uniform, stogie still in place, bobbing in the water. Apparently, the new life jackets worked.

If the Ruddy Duck on Waterlily Cove today had had a stogie, he would have looked just like that colonel of long ago. I raised my binoculars and took another look at the duck—just checking for cigars, you know. Then a few raindrops spat down, reminding me it was time to go.

I headed for the Lone Pine Tree, a shelter I have often huddled under in the rain. But the firecracker boys had been at it again the previous July, setting fire to the prairie and burning the pine tree. All that is left now is a charred trunk and some blackened, dead branches—scant shelter for a bedraggled birder with hundreds of meters yet to go. I put my head down and kept trudging. The car was a long way away.

"Let a smile be your umbrella," I muttered under my breath, pasting one onto my face as I quoted the Roaring Twenties-era song about unreasoning optimism. "Whenever skies are gray, don't you worry or fret," the song goes on. "A smile will bring the sunshine, and you'll never get wet!"

Yeah, right. Two years after that song was published, the stock market crashed. A smile is no defense against the fury of a storm. I tried to think of something else to buck myself up with.

Many years ago, my oldest son Alex went on a high-school trip to the Colorado Rockies. Early on the trip, the teacher pulled the bus into a small town and told the kids they were going to spend the night camping in the town's park. Apparently, the townies resented this, and in the middle of the night they crept into the kids' camp and stole everything that wasn't nailed down. Luckily, they didn't get much because most of the kids had locked their gear in the bus. But my son, for whatever reason, had decided to sleep with his gear tucked all around him. Alex lost everything but his sleeping bag and his boots, which he had stuck in the bottom of his sleeping bag.

The next morning, the class assessed the damage and the lessons learned. They realized they had gotten off fairly lightly, except for Alex. The teacher dipped into his emergency fund and gave Alex a little money to buy a few replacements.

My six-foot-tall son managed to buy a pair of wool socks and a long-sleeved T-shirt. When he got back in the bus, though, he discovered that a men's "size large" and a children's "size large" are two entirely different species. He learned this painful truth as the bus left town and he tried on his new shirt. He could hardly get the thing over his head. After a titanic struggle, he managed to put his arms through the sleeves and pull the shirt down. The sleeves reached his elbows and the shirt bottom fell just above his navel. But it was all he had to wear, so despite the grins of his colleagues, he kept it on.

I found out about the clothing fiasco when the kids returned home. "How did you manage with one pair of socks and such a tiny shirt?" I asked my son.

"Oh," said Alex, "I washed out my socks and shirt every night. In the morning, the clothes would be frozen solid, so I put them under my armpits to thaw out."

"Wow," I responded, "that must have been pretty miserable."

But Alex did not agree. "I had a great time," he said. The icy armpits and ill-fitting clothes were a minor blip on his radar screen. He had barely noticed, not when he had the backdrop of the Rockies to look at every day, and the wine air of the high country to breathe.

Alex knew a secret of nature that I needed to learn. Nature is not always a comfortable environment. It can be too hot or too cold, wet or parched, dirty and dangerous. But it is always beautiful and exciting. If you let a few lacks of creature comforts keep you at home ensconced in the Barcalounger, you'll miss everything.

Back at the Fill, the wind picked up and blew the rain sideways. My hat brim gave up its feeble attempt to retain its stiffness and flopped over my forehead, sending a stream of cold water down my front. By the time I got back to the car, I was as wet as the colonel who had walked off the edge of the dock.

But by golly, I was still smiling. The memories of the colonelesque Ruddy Duck—and Alex's armpits—had seen to that.

Alder leaves on ice © Jean Colley

30. Sun Worship

In the late autumn, when the air is still and conditions are right, the night fog rises from the lake and drifts through the moonlight to shroud the land. On those occasions, I like to get myself to the Fill before dawn, just as the moon slips behind the distant Olympics and the tip of the sun rises over the foothills of the Cascades. If I'm lucky, the rising sun will warm the air enough to collect the fog into one bank of cloud raised slightly above the water and positioned in perfect alignment against the backdrop of the mountains. It is then that I will see gold.

Quickly I sling my camp stool over my shoulder and hurry down the trail. I ignore the flock of Cedar Waxwings foraging in the alder and poplar tops at Leaky Pond. I can't stop today to look at every one of them to see which of the stripy juveniles are beginning to molt into the smooth adult plumage of fawn, pale yellow, and slate blue. Of all the birds in North America, I think Cedar Waxwings have the sleekest feathers, almost like they're dressed in super-suits. With their eyes masked in black, they look like avian members of the Justice League, ready to battle any evil aliens who might want to take over Earth. Today, though, the waxwings will have to save the world without me. I must hurry.

I step up my pace as I reach the Lone Pine Tree. I do not linger to scan the bushes to the east along the slough to locate the Bewick's Wren who likes to play hide-and-seek there and who starts buzzing as soon as he sees me. I'm convinced the little beggar teases me on purpose. But as my passage swirls the silver mists clinging to the ground, I tell him, "Not today. I have no time for games."

For I must reach East Point before the sun rises.

The sparrows who have favored the chicory field north of Boy Scout Pond are already awake and active. I can see them rummaging through the grass, pushing the blades aside with both feet at once as they search for seeds. I do not stop, not even when a Lincoln's Sparrow hops up on a blackberry stem and chips at me, his crest raised in alarm, his black eyes snapping. He has been back for a week now from his breeding grounds in the north. "You can just put your little crest down," I admonish as I go by without slowing. "There's no need to be scared. You know me, and I know you. We see each other every day."

At last I arrive at the overlook. Just in time. The fog bank has already risen from the water. It lies between me and the sun, just above the foothills, creating a narrow slit for the sun to shine through. The sky turns pink. The sun's corona glows. And then the light bursts forth through the clouds, carving a golden path over the water. The path widens until it becomes a road of molten gold, shimmering, beckoning. Ducks and grebes and geese paddle into the shining corridor to soak up the warmth. I cannot tell their species, for I am dazzled.

Everything in my spirit tells me to join them, to step onto the road of light and follow it. Toward what? And how? I do not know, but still I yearn. The sun enters the fog bank, the light dims, the road narrows, becomes a path, disappears. It's gone.

I sigh for the Lost Road, but the Fill is not done with me yet. As the sun creeps up a little higher, it finds a thinning in the clouds and breaks through in streaks, pouring its light upon Waterlily Cove in rays as straight as rulers, each one just touching the silvered water in gentle caress.

At the beginning of the New Kingdom in ancient Egypt, a visionary came to power. His name was Amenhotep, which meant, "[The god] Amen is content." But though the god may have been content with the king, the king was not content with Amen. He didn't like the fact that Amen was the chief god of a whole pantheon of gods too numerous to count. Amenhotep believed instead in one god, the creator of the universe and sustainer of all life: Aten, the sun-disk. To honor his beliefs, Amenhotep changed his name to Akhnaten, "I am the servant of Aten." He did more than that. He forced his people to get rid of all the other gods except Aten.

Naturally, the priests of the other gods in the kingdom were not happy with the new religion. They mourned their loss of prestige and wealth, and some of them resisted going along with the program. Oh, not openly, for Akhnaten was an absolute ruler in the truest sense and had the despot's dislike of being thwarted. But passively, the

Great Blue Heron © Kathrine Lloyd

priests of the old-time religion did everything they could to halt progress. Since the priestly caste was deeply embedded in running the day-to-day business of the kingdom, priests who wanted to erect road blocks against Akhnaten's edicts could accomplish a lot. The king, in frustration, eventually built an entirely new city in the desert, where he could be free of his pesky priests and their recalcitrance.

There, he filled his palace and grounds with tributes to Aten. Numerous examples survive, showing Akhnaten and his wife, Nefertiti, worshipping Aten. In each case, Aten is depicted as a round disk, with sun-rays coming down to bless the earth. Each ray ends in a little hand. Often, the hands are shown patting the king and queen or holding out the symbol of life, the ankh, to their faces.

I must confess I've never been that crazy about Akhnaten. He was a poor ruler and made many stupid decisions. Egypt declined under his leadership. Akhnaten's attempt to force everyone to believe as he did was coercive. Ultimately, it failed. No sooner had he died than his brand-new city was abandoned and people returned to worshipping the god of their choice.

But despite all his inadequacies, Akhnaten got one thing right. He knew the sun was the source of all life on Earth. Three thousand years later, as I stand on the shore and watch the sun's rays slant down upon the waters, I too can see in my mind's eye the rays ending in little hands, the hands patting us, blessing us, giving life to our planet. Then the clouds close up again. The little hands withdraw, the light grows dim.

The Great Blue Heron who has been watching from the cattails nearby stirs his feathers briefly and then goes back to sleep. He is not uplifted by the coming of the sun-path or the pats from solar hands, nor is he bothered by their going. For him, they are common, ordinary phenomena. He sees them often, and the moonlight, the mists, and the dawn. He lives here, surrounded by such beauty.

But I? I can only visit.

31. Light and Dark

This time of year, I always check Main Pond first thing in the morning to see if any migrating shorebirds have decided to stop for a meal on their way south. I scan the shoreline carefully. Shorebirds are cryptically colored to blend in with their surroundings, and they can be very hard to see, even when they're out in the open in plain sight.

One morning, I was slowly swiveling my scope along the shore when my eyes saw something my brain refused to process. Instead of the little brown peep I expected to see, I was looking at big red innards. I had to step back from my scope and use my regular eyes to figure out what was going on. It turned out my favorite Red-tailed Hawk had caught a coot and was disemboweling it on the edge of the pond.

This particular Red-tail has been coming here every fall for the past few years. She is a mighty hunter, catching Norway Rats that grow to the size of Volkswagens. Okay, maybe the rats aren't quite as big as cars; they only seem so when they scuttle past on the trail, giving me a jolt worse than drinking the cowboy coffee the surgeons serve on my husband's floor at the Medical Center. In my calmer moments, I admit the rats are really only the size of skateboards. Nevertheless, I wouldn't want to try to catch one. The Red-tailed Hawk, though, is supremely indifferent to the rats' size. She'll tackle anything. Once I even saw her eating a young Nutria, which she had somehow managed to haul into one of the tall cottonwoods at East Point. This year, she has branched out, enlarging her diet to include ducks. And now coots.

Red-tailed Hawk © Kathrine Lloyd

Red-tails belong to the buteo genus of raptors, a large group of hawks that eat mostly rodents. You can often see such hawks soaring over a field. When they spot a rodent, they plunge down at ferocious speed and snag their prey with talons so sharp they pierce right through an animal's hide. It is unusual to see a Red-tail catch another bird, and I wondered how this one had managed to do it.

Unconcerned by my gawking, the hawk continued to pluck her carcass. Just as she was getting to the meat of the matter, I spied a human dad and three young kids thrashing their way through the tall grass of Hunn Meadow West, heading for Main Pond. I immediately began to imitate a semaphore, trying to soundlessly telegraph to the family to keep their distance from the hawk. I didn't want them to frighten her away from her meal. But of course the kids had no way of interpreting my message, and as soon as they spotted the hawk, they made a beeline right for her.

Luckily, this particular hawk is so accustomed to people, she didn't flush. Instead, she placed one foot on her coot and glared. Between her glare and my gesticulations, the light bulb finally clicked on in the dad's brain. Recognizing his responsibilities, he shepherded the kids back onto the trail. In another few minutes, the family buzzed over to my scope to investigate the crazy woman with the blue hat and vigorous body language.

I explained that it is important to leave feeding hawks alone. Then, inspired by my memories of youthful interest in gore, I sweetened the lecture by asking the kids if they would like to get a close look through my scope. "I'm warning you, though, it's pretty gruesome," I said. "Don't look if you have a weak stomach."

Naturally, this made all the kids determined to look. "Ewww," they each said, one after another, thrilled at the sight of a coot's insides and at the real-life drama of death in the wilds of the Fill. When another troop of children showed up off-trail and began to advance on the hawk, the three new members of the Hawk Welfare League ran over and harried the newcomers back onto the trail.

It was heartwarming to see the kindness of these children and their thoughtfulness toward the hawk, but also a little scary to contrast it with their unthinking delight in death and gore. They had been so very thrilled to see the coot getting ripped apart.

"Kids don't take death, especially violent death, seriously," said my 97-year-old aunt when I told her this story. "They're too young and inexperienced. It takes an older person to really understand the value of life."

Chris Abani would no doubt agree. Abani is a poet and author from Nigeria who writes about the horrendous aftermath of the Nigerian-Biafran Civil War. As members of the Igbo tribe, Abani and his family were on the losing side. When he was 16, he was thrown in jail and tortured. Over the next few years, this happened twice more. Eventually he fled to England and later America, where he now teaches at the University of California at Riverside.

In a recent interview with Steve Scher on KUOW radio, Abani said, "A lot of my work is really against the idea of forgetting, the ways in which we want to erase difficulty, the things we don't want to remember." But, he said, his experiences in Nigeria taught him that we're never more beautiful than when we are most ugly.

"In traditional Igbo thinking, there are these beautiful birds called Cattle Egrets. You see them in swamps, and they take off in beautiful flocks across the sky. We call them *ichekelekes*. There's a song we often sing as kids, which is a spell. It is basically asking the *ichekelekes* to give you white flecks in your nails, but not to take all the darkness away. For the Igbo, the idea of beauty can only exist when there is something not beautiful. Otherwise, a thing may be pretty, but a thing that is pretty is worthless. Its only value is temporary."

Abani went on to talk about his interest in people who do terrible things—or who experience terrible things—and have to live with those memories. "When you come back from that, if you come back from that, what then do you do? In America often when we talk about healing, we think healing means the erasure of trauma. So you're only healed when there's no more trauma. Whereas where I come from, healing is learning to live with a damaged self but not to inflict any more damage. That is what is beautiful because you can never get to that part until you've seen the ugly."

Abani is correct in saying the Igbo idea of beauty is deeply un-Western. In our culture, we are sure there is an absolute ideal of beauty, even if we can't always say what it is. As far back as the ancient Greeks, we've held this precept. Socrates, for example, in 390 B.C. buttonholed a colleague named Hippias to ask him to define beauty. Hippias gave one definition after another, each of which Socrates shot down. Eventually, Hippias became so twisted up by Socrates's logical objections that he needed to go away to meditate.

I can sympathize. Socrates has that effect on me, too. Halfway through one of his dialogues, my head starts to feel like it's floating a couple of feet above my neck, and I get a strong urge to go away and meditate (preferably in the prone position with eyes closed, hoping never to encounter Socrates again). However, unlike me, Hippias was sure if he had time to think about it, he would be able to come back with a Socrates-proof definition of absolute beauty.

Both he and Socrates assumed as a given the idea that the definition of absolute beauty was out there somewhere, just waiting to be found. The idea that beauty is relative and needs ugliness in order to exist—the notion that you can find beauty only by finding ugliness—was utterly foreign to their thinking.

It is foreign to me as well. It is only at the Fill that I can even dimly begin to understand what Abani is getting at. When the Red-tailed Hawk consumed the coot, it wasn't a pretty sight. Too much of the inner coot had become outer. On the other hand, I was glad the hawk had found something to eat. And after all, the hawk must kill to survive. It has no choice.

Light and dark. I accept them both in nature. What I cannot accept is our own darkness. I suppose my difficulty lies in my belief that we humans—unlike the hawk—have volition. We can choose how to act, either for good or evil. Thus, we make our choices in the context of morality. Sometimes, we choose to hurt others, or others choose to hurt us. When that happens, we must figure out a way to live with those choices.

For many people, the best way to deal with evil in their past is to segregate it. They put it into its own compartment away from everything else and hope that it doesn't leak out to pollute other areas of their lives.

That hope was evident in letters and emails that neurobiologist André Fenton received when the media announced he had found a way to delete long-term memory. Fenton is a researcher at SUNY Downstate in Brooklyn. On a recent episode of *Nova Science Now*, he described an experiment he conducted with the help of fellow researcher Todd Sacktor. The scientists placed a rat onto a circular metallic grid. The rat was free to run around anywhere it wanted on the circle. Unfortunately for the rat, a pie slice of the circle was given an electrical charge. Every time the rat ran onto that part of the circle, it got a shock. Soon the rat learned to avoid the area. Then the rat was injected with PKMZeta, an enzyme that Sacktor suspected plays a key role in long-term memory. Sure enough, the injected rat completely lost its memory of the bad pie slice. When it was placed back onto the metal grid, it ran all over the electrified part of the circle and received many new shocks.

After the scientists' results were made public, Fenton began to receive pleas from people who had bad memories they wanted to erase. On the show, Fenton reads from some of the letters and emails he got. "If you could give me amnesia somehow, I would do it in a minute. . . ." "I would happily trade in all my memories, even the good ones, if it would erase this pain." "Sorry if I have inconve-

Western Tiger Swallowtail © Doug Parrott

nienced you in any way. I really did have a lot of accomplishments and had a lot of future potential." "I'm living in hell, and I would try anything. Please, please keep me in mind if any clinical trials..."

Fenton's voice trails off, and he gazes bemusedly into the camera. It's clear he has no idea what to make of these pleas. Fenton is a man who deeply believes that we are defined by our memories, that our very humanity depends on remembering our past experiences. "Imagine," he says, "you are an adult person, and you spent a lot of time accumulating an identity. You might not like that identity, but the very notion that you could literally remove all of it.... I don't know what you would be. I'm not sure you would be human. And I wouldn't know how to put it back."

Fenton has his own traumatic memories, but he would never erase them. Rather, he has struggled to incorporate them into his life so he can find strength from knowing who he is. Chris Abani would no doubt find great beauty in Fenton's struggle, as he does in the struggles of Nigerians who committed unspeakable atrocities during the war. When people—either victims or perpetrators—try to embrace both the good and evil memories of their lives, and through that effort find the strength to go on, they attain a plane of existence that Abani admires very much. As he puts it, for the Igbo to become beautiful, there must be the *integration* of that which is not beautiful.

Both predators and prey are an integral part of nature. It is not just that life and death, kindness and cruelty are in nature. These things *are* nature. They define nature. Indeed, nature could not exist without them.

It is easy to find divine beauty in nature, and, although I do not dwell on it, it is easy to find divine ugliness, too. I would not change anything I find in nature, whether on any particular day I see life in all its glory or death in its gore. I love the whole of nature, just the way it is, just the way I find it every day at the Fill.

Perhaps it takes divinity to love humans in the same unconditional way. Religion tells us we have that spark within us, a little piece of divinity. Maybe that is enough.

32. Music to My Ears

The Fill is never free from noise. Night or day, the city's clatter spreads over the area in continuous waves of constructed sound. For me, the noise starts as soon as I open my car door in the parking lot west of the Center for Urban Horticulture. Invariably, the first sound I hear is the SWOOSH-wickety-wickety of the CUH's fan system. In the distance, the thrum of cars over the floating bridge is a constant vibration, the heartbeat of civilized life for us ever since Henry invented a Ford. If you listen closely enough to the bridge traffic, you can hear an underlying rumble, pitched low like an elephant's infrasonic long-speech. The elephants can hear these low-frequency calls over a distance of more than 10 km. Their long-speech is a way for them to announce their presence to other animals. The elephants, at least, are communicating with each other. We are merely transporting machine and man from here to there.

As I start down the trail toward Shoveler's Pond, I hear the din of air traffic overhead, a noise I have experienced every single day at the Fill except for one: September 11, 2001. The Fill is on the flight path of the commercial jets flying in and out of Sea-Tac, and their engines are loud. But jets are not the only planes flying by. A surprising number of single-engine Cessnas pass overhead, too, taking folks for a spin, I guess. These planes are much louder than the jets, oddly. Loudest of all is the seaplane that belongs to a local pilot, who docks it near the mansions that line the eastern shore. I timed all the airplanes flying overhead today. One went by every three and a half minutes, on average.

193

Even more frequent passers-by are the joggers. Joggers, on the whole, don't make a huge racket, but I can hear them crunching the Loop Trail's gravel from a hundred meters away. It is a cheerful noise in a way, a reminder that this place is shared by people with many different interests (not just birders!), but it's human noise nonetheless. This morning the joggers have turned out early, trying to get their exercise done before the drizzle of an autumn afternoon melts them into mud puddles.

You might think all this hubbub would drown out the quieter sounds of nature, but this is not so. We hear, after all, with our brains even more than with our ears. Just as we can focus our eyes on a particular blade of grass, blocking out all others, we can tune our ears to a particular sound. As we do this, the clamor of our stressful civilization gradually fades away into the distance, and we enter the green symphony of nature.

I say "enter" because, like a musician in an orchestra, I am physically embedded in the music. It plays all around me. To my left, on Southwest Pond, is the wind section. The winds are led by an experienced Gadwall, who quacks the beat nasally. I think he prefers 2/4 time for most of his concerts. Like any good first-chair oboist, he is able to make his music heard above all the other players, not because he is the loudest, but because he is the clearest.

He is accompanied by the bagpipes of the Red-winged Blackbird who perches on his cattail podium, swells himself up with air, and lets go. Not everybody likes his song. My grandmother used to say that appreciation for bagpipes skips each generation. She loved bagpipes, my mother couldn't stand them, I adore them, and my kids think I'm nuts. I managed to drag my family only once to hear the massed bagpipers play at the Highland Games in Puyallup. I used the argument that everyone ought to attend at least one Highland Games in a lifetime.

As an aside, I used the same argument when I took them to the cat show, a dressage event, the loggers' Olympics, and the Flea Circus at Ye Olde Curiosity Shop down on the waterfront, where you can see fleas dressed in clothes. For whatever reason, nobody

Male Gadwall © Kathrine Lloyd

ever wanted to go to these venues a second time. I suppose I can vaguely understand why you might think that once you've seen one flea in a dress, you've seen them all. But I am completely baffled about why my kids say they don't ever want to hear bagpipe music again, as long as they live. It is so wild and intoxicating, so evocative of heather and plaids, I can listen to it forever. But since I can't coerce my family into going to the Highland Games anymore, I go by myself to the Fill and listen to blackbirds.

Mixed in with the woodwinds on the Loop Trail are the percussionists of the orchestra: the Downy Woodpeckers who bang out their rhythms on the nearest hollow tree, and the Song Sparrows who rattle the dry leaves of fall as they scratch through the litter, hunting for food. They are joined sometimes by the deep-throated chip of a Common Yellowthroat, the only warbler that breeds regularly at the Fill. Yellowthroats are versatile musicians, capable of singing opera arias as well as beating out drum fills. The bird who frequents the orchestra pit near Southwest Pond is highly skilled at both, but he seems to think he should divide his talent seasonally. In the spring, he sang. Now that it's fall, he's more interested in the pure rhythm of his one-note chip. I'm happy he's still playing in our symphony, but I know it won't be for long. In another week or two, he'll pack up his instruments and head south for the winter.

The brass section is a little thin this time of year. Northern Flickers cry their piercing clarion cornets from the tops of the light standards in the Dime Lot, joined by the raucous trombones of the Canada Geese in the sloughs, but the more mellow playing of the Trumpeter Swans won't be heard until late November. Swans always take the whole summer off to attend to family matters in the Far North.

I had no time to regret the absence of the trumpets, though, for the orchestra was enlarged by a guest soloist today. I heard him tuning up in the pear tree in Hunn Meadow West: the unmistakable burble of a Western Meadowlark, the most musical of all the birds at the Fill. Western Meadowlarks are birds of the farmlands, where their sober-patterned brown backs help them blend in with the loam. However, there is more to meadowlarks than plain brown houndstooth. Their bright yellow fronts, accented with a jet-black necklace, are the complete opposite of plain. I guess it must be handy for an artiste to wear two such different costumes at the same time. If he's feeling shy, he can turn his back on the audience and disappear into the background; if he's feeling more effervescent, he can flash his chest and stun all who behold him.

We often host one or two meadowlarks from November to March, but it's never a sure thing, so I was glad to hear this one had arrived. He must have been eager to play on his first day back, because he wasted little time warming up. He gave a few burbles, shook out his feathers, peeked around the curtain of leaves in the pear tree, and took one last preen. Then he was ready. Ascending to the top of his perch, he gave a nod to the oboist, and began, his song flowing out of his little body, filling the empty blue of the sky. Ah, I said to myself, it's to be a serenade. Two opening notes, descending, played forte; seven more glissando; a staccato trill; then a long pause.

Quietly, so as not to disturb the musician, I did what anyone in the cheap balcony always does after the first movement ends. I crept to a better seat. Setting up my camp stool near the pear tree, I managed to seat myself again without too many glares from the maestro. He did ruffle his feathers a little, and I feared he would stalk offstage in a huff, but then he settled back down and resumed his music.

Perhaps he enjoyed the rapturous look on the audience's face, for eventually he turned to play right at me. For a brief moment—the mere length of one bird's song—I lived on a planet graced by a binary star: the sun on high, and the meadowlark gleaming as brightly down below. The liquid notes of his serenade trilled through the dust motes puffed here and there by the wind, joining together the tangible and the invisible into one glorious whole that enwrapped every living thing. Including me.

The discordant noises of human activity dwindled from my consciousness and were gone. Here, in the orchestra of nature, there is no cacophony. There is only the harmony of birdsong, wind sighing through grass, autumn leaves breaking off from their anchor stems with a little crack and drifting down, wavelets lapping against a log, the lazy hum of insects on the wing, a beaver's slapping tail. It is peaceful, beautiful.

And it is ours whenever we choose to listen.

Western Meadowlark © Tim Kuhn

Part V
Appendices

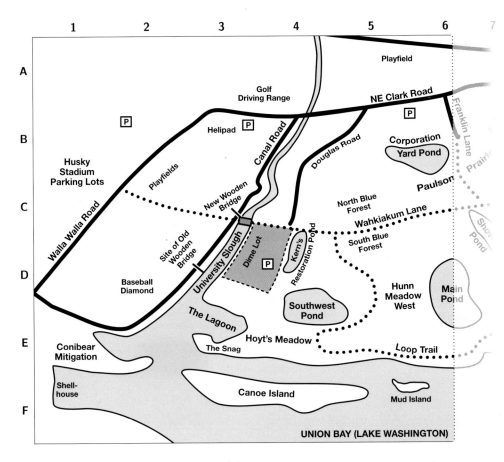

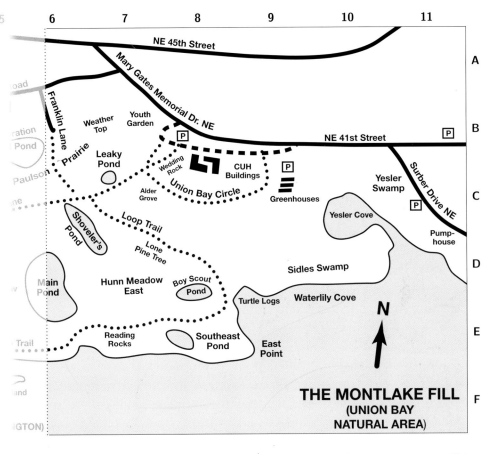

The map shows the following locations:

- **5** | **6** | **7** | **8** | **9** | **10** | **11**
- NE 45th Street
- Mary Gates Memorial Dr. NE
- Franklin Lane
- road
- ration
- Pond
- Paulson
- ne
- Weather Top
- Prairie
- Youth Garden
- Leaky Pond
- Wedding Rock
- CUH Buildings
- Union Bay Circle
- Alder Grove
- Greenhouses
- NE 41st Street
- Yesler Swamp
- Surber Drive NE
- Yesler Cove
- Pumphouse
- Shoveler's Pond
- Loop Trail
- Lone Pine Tree
- Main Pond
- Hunn Meadow East
- Boy Scout Pond
- Sidles Swamp
- Turtle Logs
- Waterlily Cove
- Reading Rocks
- Southeast Pond
- East Point
- Trail
- and
- GTON)

N

THE MONTLAKE FILL
(UNION BAY NATURAL AREA)

A. The Fill's Natural History

To birders, the Fill is a glorious nature reserve, with widely varied micro-habitats that regularly attract more than 130 different species of birds each year. To birds, the Fill must seem an island of wild nature in a sea of cement, a haven where they can overwinter, breed in the summer, or just grab a bite to eat during migration.

To the folks who run this place, though—the faculty and staff of the UW Botanic Gardens—it is a 75-acre laboratory, a place for ecological experiment and education.

The experiment began in 1971, when the Montlake Landfill officially closed and the university decided to set it aside as a natural area. Prior to its life as a landfill, the site was underwater, just another bay in Lake Washington. When the lake was lowered an average of nine feet in 1916—upon the opening of the Montlake Cut—a wetland emerged. The City of Seattle eyed this wasteland on the outskirts of Laurelhurst and decided it would make a great dump. From 1926 until 1971, tons of garbage and construction waste were trucked here. After the dump closed, it was covered with a thin layer of clay and soil and planted with European grasses. The laboratory was now open for business.

Nature was the first "scientist" to go to work in the lab. The flat land began to change shape, sinking in some places as the peat underneath the garbage compressed, and rising in others as the spongy soil was pushed up. Ponds formed in the depressions, and new plants began to grow from seeds brought in by waterfowl, songbirds, and wind.

Unfortunately, few of these colonizing plants were native. The thin soil that city workers had spread over the dump was just too poor in nutrients to sustain them. As large-scale native plant recruitment failed, non-native invasive plants moved in. A survey conducted in 1986 documented 150 flowering plants, the majority of

Montlake Landfill in the 1950s © Seattle Municipal Archives

which were non-native. Among the most aggressive were Himalayan Blackberry and Purple Loosestrife. Year by year, these invasives took over more and more of the site. At their worst, blackberry covered nearly 40 percent of the land, and loosestrife choked every pond. The experiment—to see what would happen to a landfill after it closed—was producing unwanted results.

In 1990, restoration ecology faculty and students began to fight back. They mowed and hand-pulled the blackberry and loosestrife and replanted plots of land with native plants. They built up mounds in the compacted soils of a former parking lot to create microclimates that would be helpful for Garry Oak and native grasses and sedges. They laid down sheet mulch to increase soil moisture around native saplings. They planted innumerable willow stakes to shade out non-native plants.

Eventually, these experiments gave rise to a new branch of science at the UW: restoration ecology. Under the direction of professor Kern

Montlake Fill today, a mix of prairie, riparian, and pond habitats © Doug Parrott

Ewing, the program has restored more than 14 acres of native plants at Union Bay Natural Area (the UW's official name for the Montlake Fill). In the course of this restoration work, students have developed many techniques to control invasives, techniques which are now being used by other groups interested in native plant restoration throughout the region.

Non-native plants still dominate much of the ecology of the Fill, but there are no more monocultures of invasives. Instead, there is a diverse mix of swamp, wetland, prairie, and riparian habitats that continue to evolve to favor the survival of more native plants. The plants, in turn, attract more diverse species of birds. In the past three or four years, we have seen an exponential rise of Savannah Sparrow populations in the prairies. Warbling Vireos, Willow Flycatchers, and Western Wood-Pewees have bred in the riparian areas. Virginia Rails are doing well in the marshlands. Gadwalls, Cinnamon Teals, and Wood Ducks are having great breeding success in the secluded ponds on the site and in Yesler Swamp. On the down side, however, shorebirds which used to be present in famously high numbers during migration have pretty much stopped coming except for a few stragglers, as the open mudflats which used to ring the ponds have given way to drier land supporting thick bushes and scrub.

Restoration continues to be an ongoing, uphill battle. Himalayan Blackberry is still omnipresent, though much reduced. Left to itself, it would again take over much of the Fill. English Ivy would also do its best to dominate. On the plus side, Purple Loosestrife is no longer a problem. It is now controlled very effectively by a European beetle introduced by the state and county. On the minus side, a new loosestrife—Yellow Garden Loosestrife—has appeared in the marshes. It has no known natural controls. Scotch Broom is on the rise in the prairies; and milfoil, non-native iris, and water lilies threaten to clog the swamp and marshes.

The thing about restoration ecology, you see, is that you can't just go into a site once and pull out every invasive plant. Seeds from these invasives can lie dormant in the soil for years, just waiting for their chance to sprout. Birds bring in non-native seeds and continuously

Lincoln's Sparrow © Doug Parrott

deposit them all over the site. Will we ever get rid of all the invasive species? The experiments conducted here give us a sobering answer: Probably not. But the research done here also proves that with effort and resources, we can control the invaders enough to allow the native plants—and the animals that depend on them—to thrive.

And that is the biggest experiment of them all, for as the world becomes more interconnected, native biota everywhere are under pressure. What happens here—both good and bad—happens everywhere. What we do here to preserve native species matters.

B. Inspiration

Some years ago, I led a Seattle Audubon birding trip to eastern Washington. We were driving in a caravan of cars down the Yakima Canyon when I spotted another caravan pulled off the side of the road. Everyone in that party was gazing through binoculars at the cliff nearby. Thinking quickly, I swerved onto the pullout, leaped out of my car, and ran up to join them. "What are you seeing?" I panted, thinking perhaps it was an owl. Great Horned Owls are known to nest in the volcanic basalt of these cliffs, and that would have been a great trip bird for us.

The people lowered their binoculars and stared at us eager birders clustered all around them. Finally one said, "We're geologists. We're looking at rock strata."

I have often commented how wonderful it is anytime we discover a window that allows us to view nature. I have to admit, though, I never thought of a geology window before. Not that I'm objecting, mind you. I'm celebrating the discovery of another way to be in nature. For nature offers us more than just a window through which to peek into a wild realm we no longer occupy. Nature also opens a *door* for us into that world.

When we cross the threshold, we change. We are not just in another world, we are of it. For many of us, the experience is so overwhelming, we simply must let our feelings out—to share with others, perhaps, or merely to keep from exploding ourselves.

For two years now, whenever I have noticed someone at the Fill who seems transfixed by its beauty, I ask if he or she would like a page in my book to express those feelings. The poetry, paintings, photos, and stories that follow are the result.

I hope they inspire you, too, to enter the wild world of nature and discover what lies within.

Mt. Rainier from Union Bay © Molly Hashimoto

Heron Who Carries Us

by Tina Blade

Born of mudflat, saltmarsh,
nimbostratus, her gray-blue spirit
is a spirit sobered
by waiting.

Such a keenly evolved patience —
standing in the rain
on her one-stilt leg.
Or watching:
   the incandescent
   bead of her eye
   becomes the flash
   of a fish
   on the tip of her knife-stab beak.

When from the marsh she rises
and takes her throaty squawk with her
we stop —

feel in our chests
the huge intake
of breath, the slow beat
of wings
carving
uplift from air.

Legs behind her —
a slow-motion diver
into sky.
Such dignity
holds us speechless, carries us

clear

above the dark
tips of trees —

above fences, green fields,
and the river's
satin curve.

We watch
till we can't see her —
till the last hill and last light
have taken her

back
into the broken
blue egg
of the earth.

Wilson's Phalaropes © Doug Parrott

Seeing and photographing birds like these is why I come to the Fill. It is a peaceful and calming place, where anyone can come to get away from the hustle and bustle of everyday life in this complex world. And just look what you can find sometimes, right here in the middle of a large city!—*Doug Parrott*

Least Sandpiper © Dennis Paulson

Juvenile Red-necked Phalarope © Alexandra MacKenzie

Choosing Sides

a prose poem by Amy Davis

A sunrise of butter-gold opens the first warm day since last August. I am up at 5:00, boiling water, cracking eggs, spooning raisins into oatmeal. I eat swiftly, grab binoculars, and rush off to the Montlake Fill. In June, I live by bird time.

In the western meadow, Scotch Broom erupts in egg-yolk yellow. They're a vicious, greedy bunch, those Brooms, an unwanted transplant from somewhere afar, bent on land-grabbing wherever they can. They swarm about the fields, while dragonflies pedal in and land low on horsetails. In the marsh, Virginia Rails ring like alarm clocks. Blackbirds yodel in the cattails. I sit here all morning, waiting for sounds, watching for birds, wildly choosing sides.

I try in vain to remain neutral, an outside observer passing through. But my eyes are wary for River Otters, once my favorite of water creatures. I used to delight when their noses and tails popped up like bubbles in the pond. Now I watch with caution: otters rob grebes' nests and dine on scrambled eggs for breakfast. I always side with the eggs.

Here in this urban wildlife zone, I can't make peace with the laws of nature. The otters must eat, the grebes must hatch, I don't know who to hope for. Sometimes I think I've failed at birding. I cringe to watch a Red-tailed Hawk rip the guts of a rat. Or a hapless coot struggle in the talons of an eagle. I anthropomorphize off the charts: project my feelings, choose sides, reel with the bare-bones shock of nature.

A mother Mallard crosses the trail, leading her brood on a hunt for bugs. The little ones run on water, skate on lilies, skitter in pools of mud. My friend Connie, across the field, waves me toward a meadowlark concert. I root for everyone on mornings like this. But mostly, I root for the Fill itself—a deeply scarred piece of land balanced on caverns of human debris. But the Fill thrives anyway. I don't know how. Starbursts of Salsify sun in the meadows, Cooper's Hawks prowl the trails. I root for everyone on days like this. Everyone's on our side.

Killdeer and chick © Kathrine Lloyd

Green Heron © Marc Hoffman

Yesler Swamp ©Jean Colley

A New Perspective

by Alex Sidles

I didn't really understand the Montlake Fill until I began kayaking there. Floating in the middle of Union Bay, I can see the cattails growing in an almost unbroken ark from the Arboretum to the tip of Foster Island, over to the Museum of History and Industry, across the Montlake Cut to the University's boathouses, and east across the Fill itself, to where the waterfront houses begin. Seeing the cattails from this perspective, as one continuous growth, makes it obvious that the whole area is actually one cohesive habitat.

It was a surprise to me when I realized this. Visiting all these places on land over the years, I had always thought of them as entirely separate from one another: The Montlake Fill was its own little universe, the boathouses were their own little world, and so on. It wasn't until I saw these places together at the same time, which can best be done from the water, that I realized they are all the same.

They may fall under the jurisdiction of different government agencies and private owners, they may serve different functions, but ecologically there is no difference between the Fill and the other lands that ring the bay. The only divisions between them are mental divisions that we assign them based on their different human purposes—the plants and animals see them all as one.

If you love the Montlake Fill, take a trip to see it from the water someday. You don't have to go by kayak; any craft will do. You'll learn the Fill is a lot bigger than you thought.

Rufous Hummingbird and fireweed © Penny Bolton

Loop Trail in winter © Mary Lou Smith

The Gathering

by Dianna L. Moore

It begins with just a few birds
silently slipping into the trees across the street.

Soft mutterings swell into chatter as more join the group
and the passing day is discussed—who saw what
and where to find the good food.

As the light slowly fades, their numbers grow.

Soon there are hundreds adorning the power lines
and overflowing into the nearby trees.

Some still circle around the area; could they perhaps be lower
in the social order, this year's kids?

Their raucous voices overwhelm the senses
so that even the less discerning humans take notice.

Uneasy remarks are made about Hitchcock's *The Birds*
by those who lack understanding. "It's just the evening gathering
of a murder of crows," I explain.

Just before darkness envelops the sky
they finish their business and head for their roost,
still hurling insults. . .or so it sounds to our untrained ears.

East Basin Memories

by Melinda Rahskopf Bronsdon

During the war years, my parents had a victory garden. We lived in Laurelhurst over by the beach club, and my dad was on the UW faculty. Our plot was long and narrow, over on the east side of the landfill. It ran from the street down to the water's edge. We went down in the evenings to weed and water. Dad carried buckets of water from the lake, and Mother and I dipped out one coffee can of water for each plant.

I was under five years old, but it was the beginning of my lifetime interest in plants and gardens. My mother would hoe the rows; I was too young. Mother hated the gardening. She grew up on a farm in eastern Washington and had had too much of the farm work while growing up!

I fondly remember shelling peas and canning produce with Mother. Early on, we also received boxes of fruit from my grandparents' ranch in Maryhill, and I learned from my mother how to can fruit. We had a frightening pressure cooker that whistled and sputtered and let off steam.

After the war, there was a commercial cannery in Kenmore. You took your own produce there in the morning and did the preparation yourself, skinning and slicing the fruit and vegetables and loading the cans, adding the sugar or salt or spice on top. Only the adults were allowed inside; there was a small area outside the building where kids could wait and play. After we left by noon, the cannery processed the cans, and we went back the following day to pick them up. They were stamped on the lid with the name of the contents, the date, and your number.

I don't remember when the victory gardens stopped but probably by the late 1940s because the UW built family student housing there for all the returning veterans who came to college. Now the area has returned to nature, but in my memory, I can still see the rows and rows of our garden.

C. Birds of Montlake Fill

I am often asked why I go to the Fill nearly every day. More than anything else, I go because every day is different, and I never know what I will find. I do know I will find at least one surprise, no matter how often I visit. Sometimes the surprise is a new behavior by a bird, increasing my knowledge of its personality, deepening my intimacy with this place. Often, though, the surprise is a totally new species. Birds fly, and they can show up almost anywhere. Furthermore, habitats change rapidly at the Fill, as the spongy land sinks in some places and gets wetter, while the land rises elsewhere and becomes drier. New plants move in, attracting new species and discouraging the old stand-bys. All this means that the list of bird species at the Fill continues to get longer, ever since record-keeping began in the 1890s. The following list has been updated from its first appearance in *In My Nature* in 2009. It has been compiled with the help of numerous birders over the years (see list of contributors at the end). Despite the great care we have all taken to be complete and accurate, mistakes might have been made (as the politicians say). I encourage readers to contact me with additional sightings and/or corrections.

The total number of bird species ever seen at the Fill is 247.

GREATER WHITE-FRONTED GOOSE Uncommon winter resident. More common as migrant. High count of 50 flying over, May 4, 2010 (*CSi*).

EMPEROR GOOSE Rare visitor. One August 1988 (*KA*).

SNOW GOOSE Occasional winter resident and spring migrant. High count: 200 flying over, October 8, 2007 (*CSi*). Most recent sightings: One February 9 and 10, 2010 (*SLC, CSi*). Two April 19 and 20, 2010 (*CSi*).

BRANT Rare visitor. One for half a day, late March 1986 (*KA*).

CACKLING GOOSE Uncommon winter visitor and migrant, sometimes in large flocks.

CANADA GOOSE Common resident and breeder.

MUTE SWAN Occasional introduced resident and breeder. Three May 15, 1980; three September 29 and November 1, 1980; two December 11, 1980; two with young May 27, 1982; four December 27, 1982; one April 8, 1983; two with young June 11, 1983 (*ER*). Two attempted to nest, July 1989 (*CSi*). A pair with two young July 16, 1995 (*DP*). Latest sighting: one December 17, 1998 (*WOS/TAv*).

Pied-billed Grebe on nest © Thomas Sanders

TRUMPETER SWAN   Rare winter visitor. Two flew over, December 15, 1984 (*KA*). One October 16, 1998 (*BV*). Two November 5, 2007 (*WOS/NLr*). One November 10, 2007 (*WOS/JB*). Fifteen arrived December 22, 2008; eleven (eight adults, three immatures) stayed on the lake for months. Three immatures returned as adults in 2009 and 2010. Six adults appeared January 1, 2011 and stayed until spring (*CSi*).

TUNDRA SWAN   Rare winter visitor. Reported in the 1940s (*HL*). One late October through mid-November 1970 (*FK*). Three December 17, 1998 (*WOS/TAv*). One near shellhouse December 22, 2008 (*CSi*). Twenty flying over, March 6, 2010 (*CSi*).

WOOD DUCK   Common (though sometimes reclusive) resident and breeder. Bred more commonly in the 1940s (*HL*), diminished after habitat loss, now common again as swampy woodlands increase. Unusual sighting: mother with nine babies May 28, 2006 (*CSi*).

GADWALL   Common resident and breeder.

EURASIAN WIGEON   Uncommon winter resident. Usually one or two present each year.

AMERICAN WIGEON   Common winter resident, rare in summer.

AMERICAN BLACK DUCK   Rare introduced visitor. One male December 29, 1979 through June 10, 1980; one male November 7, 1981 (*ER*).

MALLARD   Common resident and breeder.

BLUE-WINGED TEAL   Regular spring and summer visitor.

CINNAMON TEAL   Uncommon summer resident and breeder; becoming more common over past three years. Occasional winter resident.

NORTHERN SHOVELER   Common winter resident and sometime summer breeder. Most recent breeding record: spring 2011 (*KL*).

NORTHERN PINTAIL   Uncommon visitor, sometime winter resident; recorded every month (*ER, CSi*).

GREEN-WINGED TEAL   Common winter resident, returning by late July (*BtW*). Occasional summer resident (*ER*). Eurasian subspecies (Common Teal) is a rare winter visitor: One between January 27 and April 27, 2000 (*CSi*). One January 4 to May 7, 2001 (*BV; WOS/TAv, JB*). One January 11, 2004 (*SMa*). One arrived January 29, 2010 and stayed some months; returned December 5, 2010 and stayed until April 26, 2011 (*CSi*).

CANVASBACK   Uncommon winter resident.

REDHEAD   Found regularly in the fall (usually most common in November) during the early 1970s (*ER, DP*). Now uncommon visitor in winter or spring. Most recent records: One overwintered 2008-2009 (*CSi, EvH*). One December 29, 2009 (*CSi*). At least six January 27, 2010, staying for several days (*EvH, CSi*).

TUFTED DUCK   Rare visitor. One May 3, 1996 (*WOS/JHe*).

RING-NECKED DUCK   Common winter resident.

GREATER SCAUP   Uncommon winter resident.

LESSER SCAUP   Common winter resident.

SURF SCOTER   Rare visitor. One adult male February 11, 1980; one immature male October 7, 1980 (*MC*). One immature October 8, 2009 (*EvH*).

WHITE-WINGED SCOTER   Rare visitor. Nine September 22, 1939 (*MC*).

LONG-TAILED DUCK   Rare visitor. One March 26, 1981 (*ER*). One March 4, 1990 (*DP*). One October 29, 2006 (*WOS/JBr*).

BUFFLEHEAD   Common winter resident. Occasionally one stays through the summer.

COMMON GOLDENEYE   Uncommon winter resident and rare summer visitor. Two records for June: one in 1981, one in 1983 (*ER*).

BARROW'S GOLDENEYE   Rare visitor. One January 21, 1981 (*ER*). Two April 25, 1988 (*KA*). One February 21, 2007 (*BtW*). One December 31, 2009 (*AdS*).

HOODED MERGANSER   Common winter resident and uncommon summer breeder.

COMMON MERGANSER   Uncommon winter resident and common spring migrant, as large numbers stage in the lake and bay before migrating.

RED-BREASTED MERGANSER   Rare spring migrant. More common in the 1940s in the fall (*HL*). Five in April 1982 (*ER*). One April 15, 2008; two April 19, 2009 (*CSi*). Two October 8, 2009 (*EvH*).

RUDDY DUCK   Uncommon winter resident, formerly abundant: 500 January 1983 (*ER*). Rare summer visitor: one July 5 to 26, 1980; one August 19 to 29, 1980; three August 5, 1982; one August 12, 1982 (*ER*). Successful nesting 1987 through 1989 (*KA*). One July 25 through September 18, 2008 (*CSi*).

RING-NECKED PHEASANT   Formerly common resident and breeder, now extirpated. Last reported: One vocalizing July 12, 2009 (*GOO*). One seen near Yesler Swamp July 21, 2009 (*MaH*).

CALIFORNIA QUAIL   Formerly common resident and breeder, now extirpated, although rare visitors still appear occasionally. Most recent sightings: One April 8, 2009 (*DPa*). One calling May 5 through 9, 2009; one February 2 and 19, 2010 (*CSi*).

NORTHERN BOBWHITE   Rare visitor. One September 11, 1997 (*WOS/TAv*).

COMMON LOON   Rare visitor. Reported regularly in the winter in the 1940s (*HL*). One flyover July 16, 1980; one in Union Bay April 17, 1982 (*ER*). One flyover April 16, 2008 (*WOS/TAv*). One in Union Bay October 30, 2008 (*CSi*).

RED-THROATED LOON   One March 20,1943 (*ER*). Occasional winter visitor (*DP*).

PIED-BILLED GREBE   Common resident and breeder.

HORNED GREBE   Uncommon winter resident.

RED-NECKED GREBE   Rare visitor. One November 1979; one June 7, 1982 (*ER*). One September 4, 2007; one October 2, 2007; one December 1, 2007 (*BtW*). Two November 27, 2008 (*CSi*). Two December 23, 2008 (*EvH*). One February 14, 19, 21, 2009 (*EvH, CSi*). One March 13 and 29, 2009 (*EvH*). One February 3, 2010 (*CSi*). One in breeding plumage April 30, 2011; one August 27, 2011 (*CSi*).

EARED GREBE   Rare visitor. More common in the 1940s, arriving in fall (*HL*). Occasional winter visitor in 1970s (*FK*). One February 28, 1981 (*ER*). Two October 28, 1986; one September 18, 1989 (*KA*).

WESTERN GREBE   Uncommon winter visitor and migrant.

CLARK'S GREBE   Rare visitor. Two calling July 21, 1989 (*KA*).

DOUBLE-CRESTED CORMORANT   Common winter resident.

AMERICAN BITTERN   Former uncommon resident and breeder (*HL*), now scarce. Most recent sightings: One September 11, 2006 (*MtB*). One February 4, 2007; one October 5, 2007 (*BtW*). One July 25, 2008 (*CSi*). One July 7, 2009 (*KL*). One August 17, 2009 (*CSi*).

GREAT BLUE HERON   Common resident and occasional breeder. Successful nesting in 1989 (*KA*). New heronry established on UW campus near Drumheller Fountain 2009; more than 30 nests reported in 2011.

GREAT EGRET   Rare visitor. One June 16 to July 2, 1987 (*KA*). Two May 15, 2000 (*WOS/RR*).

CATTLE EGRET   Rare late fall or winter visitor. One November 11 through 18, 2004 (*WOS/FB, KAn; MtB, CSi*). One November 5 through 9, 2007 (*BtW; WOS/NLr, CSi, CPe*).

GREEN HERON   Uncommon summer resident and breeder. First state nesting record, 1939 (*HL*).

BLACK-CROWNED NIGHT-HERON   Rare visitor. Two reported in the 1940s (*HL*). One December 5, 1974 (*FK*). One August 15 to September 3, 1987 (*KA*).

TURKEY VULTURE   Uncommon spring and fall migrant, only flyovers. Most recent sightings: Eighteen September 26, 2008; two April 8, 2009 (*CSi*). Two April 2, 2011 (*PD, WW*). One June 7, 2011 (*CSi*).

OSPREY   Uncommon summer visitor. One or two come by regularly in summer and stay briefly to catch fish.

GOLDEN EAGLE   Rare visitor. One March 21, 2010 (*CSi*).

BALD EAGLE   Common resident and breeder. Current nest on Talaris site nearby.

Bald Eagle © Tim Kuhn

NORTHERN HARRIER Common visitor in the 1940s (*HL*); only single visitors now, mostly in fall. Most recent sightings: One May 6, 2009 (*EvH*). One August 12, 2009 (*CBB*). One flyover, April 12, 2010 (*EvH*). One adult male flyover April 16, 2010 (*CSi*). One July 17, 2011 (*KAS, EW*)

SHARP-SHINNED HAWK Occasional visitor, more common as fall migrant or in winter.

COOPER'S HAWK Uncommon visitor, more common in fall and winter. One summered in 1985 and 1987 (*KA*).

NORTHERN GOSHAWK Rare winter visitor. One February 3 and 19, 1972 (*FK*). Several sightings in winter of 1981 to 1982 (*ER*).

RED-SHOULDERED HAWK Rare visitor. One August 7, 2006 (*CCx*). One February 5, 2010 (*CSi*).

RED-TAILED HAWK One to three usually present in spring, fall, and winter. One pair year-round resident in 2008 (*CSi*).

ROUGH-LEGGED HAWK Rare visitor. Two flew over in late October 1974 (*KA*). One February 3, 1982 (*ER*).

AMERICAN KESTREL Formerly regular fall visitor (*KA*), now rare. Most recent sightings: One September 27, 2009 (*HG, HN*). One September 11, 2010; one April 4, 2011 (*CSi*).

MERLIN Occasional visitor year-round.

PEREGRINE FALCON Occasional visitor year-round.

VIRGINIA RAIL Uncommon summer resident and breeder, becoming more common. At least nine nested in various ponds, coves, and shoreline cattails in 2011 (*CSi*).

SORA Uncommon summer resident and breeder. Most recent sightings: One May 26, 2010 (*EvH*). One August 28, 2010 (*JT and many observers*). One September 7 (*CSi*). One September 10, 2010 (*CSi, KAS*). One April 23, 2011 (*KAS, HG, HN*). One May 1, 2011 (*CSi*). One juvenile August 20, 2011 (*TK*).

AMERICAN COOT Common resident and rare breeder.

SANDHILL CRANE Rare visitor, only flyovers. Two October 12, 1980 (*ER*). Three September 17, 2007 (*WOS/BtW*). One September 27, 2009 (*EvH*).

BLACK-BELLIED PLOVER Regular migrant in 1940s (*HL*). Now rare. Two May 14, 1979; one May 5, 1980, one April 6 and 9, 1983; August 1 and 8, 1983; one first week of September 1983 (*ER*). One September 12, 1985 (*KA*). One April 22, 2004 (*WOS/EH*).

AMERICAN GOLDEN-PLOVER Rare migrant. One September 14, 1981 (*DP*).

SEMIPALMATED PLOVER Rare migrant. High count of five May 13, 1986 (*KA*). One May 31, 1996; one July 17, 1997 (*CM*). One August 6, 2000 (*WOS/JB*). Three August 7, 2000 (*CSi*). One April 29, 2007 (*WOS/PC, MEg*). One May 8, 2008 (*BV*).

KILLDEER Common resident and breeder.

BLACK-NECKED STILT Rare migrant. One May 12, 1988 (*KA*). One April 29, 1993 (*WOS/TB*).

AMERICAN AVOCET Rare migrant. One May 28, 1980 (*ER*). One March 31, 1988 (*KA*). One May 30, 1998 (*WOS/BB*).

SPOTTED SANDPIPER Uncommon resident and regular migrant. Bred commonly in the 1940s (*HL*) and annually in the 1970s (*KA*). Last reported nesting: 1987 (*KA*).

SOLITARY SANDPIPER Rare spring and fall migrant; usually one present briefly each year.

GREATER YELLOWLEGS Occasional spring migrant, uncommon fall migrant.

LESSER YELLOWLEGS Occasional spring migrant, uncommon fall migrant.

UPLAND SANDPIPER Rare migrant. One August 18, 1998 (*WOS/TAv*).

WHIMBREL Rare visitor. One May 4, 1974 (*FK*). One in late September 1975 (*KA*). One May 3, 1981 (*ER*). One April 30, 1994 (*WOS/DMc*).

SANDERLING Rare migrant. Two juveniles September 25, 1986 (*KA*).

SEMIPALMATED SANDPIPER Formerly uncommon but regular fall migrant, now rare. Six spring records: One May 25, 1974 (*FK*). One May 13, 1976 (*DP*). One May 8, 1982 (*ER*). One May 10 to 12, 1996 (*CM; WOS/JiF*). One May 10, 2000 (*WOS/TAv*). Most recent fall records: One July 22, 2008 (*EvH*). One July 23, 2010 (*EvH,KAS*). One August 15, 2010 (*CSi, DPa*). One August 8, 2011 (*CSi*).

WESTERN SANDPIPER   Common spring and fall migrant.

LEAST SANDPIPER   Common spring and fall migrant. Rare winter visitor: one January 9, 1982; one February 5 through 9, 1982 (*ER*).

BAIRD'S SANDPIPER   Rare fall migrant. Highest count: three September 10, 1989 (*KA*). One spring record: May 9, 1985 (*KA*). Most recent sightings: August 14, 2007 (*CSi*); August 15 and 19, 2007 (*BtW*).

PECTORAL SANDPIPER   Rare spring and fall migrant, although usually at least one is present briefly each year. Slightly more common in fall than in spring. Most recent sightings: One July 22, 2008 (*EvH*). One May 15, 2009 (*CSi*). One September 12 and 13, 2010 (*CSi, TK, KAS*).

SHARP-TAILED SANDPIPER   Rare migrant. One September 29, 1996 (*WOS/KA*), last seen October 14, 1996 (*CM*).

DUNLIN   Occasional winter visitor, occasional spring migrant. High count: more than 40, November 5, 2006 (*CSi*).

RUFF   Rare visitor. One September 1, 1995 (*WOS/RSt*).

STILT SANDPIPER   Rare visitor. One July 29, 1965 (*FK*). One August 30 to September 8, 1981 (*ER*). Two September 13, 1981 (*EH*). One August 29, 1989 (*KA*). One August 31 to September 1, 1996 (*CM, CSi*). One August 17 and 18, 1997 (*CM, BV*).

BUFF-BREASTED SANDPIPER   Rare visitor. One stayed seven days, reported in the 1940s (*HL*).

SHORT-BILLED DOWITCHER   Rare migrant.

LONG-BILLED DOWITCHER   Uncommon spring migrant, common fall migrant.

WILSON'S SNIPE   Uncommon fall, winter, and spring resident.

WILSON'S PHALAROPE   Uncommon spring migrant; usually at least one present each season. High counts: Four June 5, 2003 (*WOS/MtB*). One female, two males May 24, 2008 (*CSi*). One fall record: August 1, 1987 (*KA*).

RED-NECKED PHALAROPE   Rare migrant. More common in the 1940s (*HL*). High count: 65 on May 20, 1980 (*ER*). Most recent records: One August 9, 2009 (*EvH*). One August 20, 2009 (*KL, JP*). Two August 21, 2009, remaining for some days; four August 23, 2009 (*CSi, KAS, EvH*). One August 11, 2010 (*DPa, CSi*).

BONAPARTE'S GULL   Formerly common spring and fall migrant, now rare. Most recent sightings: One June 4, 2008 (*DPa*). One August 29, 2009 (*EvH*). One September 24, 2009; one October 10, 2009; four October 31, 2009 (*CSi*). One November 11, 2010 (*JeB*). One November 16, 2010; one in breeding plumage April 24, 2011 (*CSi*).

BLACK-HEADED GULL   Rare visitor. One April 19, 1998 (*SMa, CSi*).

FRANKLIN'S GULL   One reported in the 1940s (*HL*) for first county record. Occasional in fall (*DP*). Most recent sighting: one August 29, 2009 (*EvH*).

MEW GULL   Common fall and winter visitor.

RING-BILLED GULL   Common winter resident, less common in summer.

WESTERN GULL   Rare visitor. One March 11, 1988 (*KA*). One January 21, 2009 (*CSi*). One February 11, 2009 (*EvH*). One January 1, 2010; one April 18, 2010; one January 26, 2011 (*CSi*).

CALIFORNIA GULL   Uncommon fall and winter visitor.

HERRING GULL   Occasional fall and winter visitor. Most recent sighting: February 28, 2011 (*CSi*).

THAYER'S GULL   Occasional winter visitor. One late, May 31, 1982 (*ER*). Most recent sighting: January 9, 2011 (*CSi*).

GLAUCOUS-WINGED GULL   Common resident. Nested in summers of 1984 and 1985 (*ER*).

CASPIAN TERN   Uncommon summer visitor, though present every summer.

BLACK TERN Rare visitor. One August 22, 1972 (*FK*). Two May 28, 1975; one late May 1976; one early June 1977 (*KA*). One June 8, 1980 (*ER*). One May 14, 2000 (*CSi*).

COMMON TERN Rare fall migrant. Eighteen August 19, 1980; two September 2, 1980; 25 September 13, 1982 (*ER*). Flock of 37 September 2, 1985; another flock of 26 September 3, 1989 (*KA*). Three September 10, 2003 (*WOS/SMa*).

ROCK PIGEON Common resident in University Village, commonly seen as flyovers and as foragers in playfields and in burns.

BAND-TAILED PIGEON Uncommon resident in the 1980s (*DP*), now uncommon visitor. Possible nesting: May 2009 (*CSi*).

EURASIAN COLLARED-DOVE Rare visitor. One May 10, 2008 (*CSi*). One April 18, 2009 (*GOO*). One April 20, 2009; one April 12, 2010; one July 29 and 31, 2010; two March 11, 2011 (*CSi*).

MOURNING DOVE Uncommon visitor. Most recent sightings: One seen off and on throughout July, August 2009 (*EvH, CSi, and many observers*). One December 23, 2009 (*JeB*). One May 24, 2010 (*CSi*). Two May 26 and 29, 2010 (*EvH, KAS*) and again on June 15, 2010 (*CSi*). One October 29, 2010 (*KAS*). One May 7, 2011 (*EvH*).

BARN OWL Rare visitor. One October 1972 (*KA*). One September 4 and 16, 1980; one March 26, 1981; two May 4, 1981 (*ER*). One seen regularly in late July 2008 (*CSi*). One October 9, 2008 (*MtB*). One August 16, 2009 (*DPa, KAS, HG, HN*). One September 12, 2009 (*CSi and many observers*).

GREAT HORNED OWL Rare visitor. One March 18, 2007 (*MFM, CSi*). One November 7, 2007 (*MtB, TM*).

SNOWY OWL Rare visitor. Two wintered in 1973 to 1974 (*FK*). One seen in winter of 1975 to 1976 and 1977 to 1978 (*KA*). One March 3 to 9, 1979 (*ER*). One December 11, 2005 (*WOS/MtD*).

SHORT-EARED OWL Occasional visitor, now rare. One November 1992; one November 1995; one October 1996 (*BV*). One October 13, 1997 (*WOS/TAv*). One November 8, 1999 (*WOS/ED*). One October 19, 2006 (*BtW*). One November 25, 2006 (*WOS/TAv*). One January 17, 2007 (*BtW*). One November 13, 2008 (*EvH*).

NORTHERN SAW-WHET OWL Rare visitor. One October 14, 1995 (*WOS/PHa*). One November 28 through December 3, 2009 (*KAS, CSi, JAS, and many observers*).

COMMON NIGHTHAWK Common summer resident in the 1940s (*HL*). Nesting reported in the early 1970s (*FK*). Now rare migrant. One June 3, 1988 (*KA*). One September 20, 2002 (*WOS/SMa*). One August 27, 2004 (*WOS/SMa*). One September 18 and 19, 2006 (*WOS/PCr; EvH*). One June 8, 2008 (*MtB*). One September 11, 2010 (*CSi*).

COMMON POORWILL Rare visitor. One May 20 to 25, 2006 (*WOS/LKi, AdS*).

BLACK SWIFT Uncommon spring migrant and summer visitor.

VAUX'S SWIFT Common summer visitor.

ANNA'S HUMMINGBIRD None noted prior to the early 1980s (*ER, KA*). Now common resident and breeder.

RUFOUS HUMMINGBIRD Reported in summers in 1940s (*HL*). Rare visitor (*ER*) prior to the explosive growth of Himalayan Blackberry in the 1990s. Uncommon summer resident and breeder in the 1990s. Now much scarcer visitor and sometime breeder. Most recent sightings: June 14, 2011; July 5, 2011 (*CSi*). One July 17, 2011 (*KAS, EW*). One July 27, 2011 (*CSi*).

BELTED KINGFISHER Common resident.

LEWIS'S WOODPECKER Rare visitor. One September 3 to 10, 1984 (*ER*). One flying over August 25, 1987; one September 1, 1989 (*KA*).

RED-BREASTED SAPSUCKER Rare visitor. One early November 1982 (*ER*). One September 17, 1987 (*KA*). One December 5 and 9, 2007 (*BtW*). One March 25, 2009 (*EvH*). One

November 11, 2009 (*JeB*). One December 26, 2009 (*CSi*). One January 25, 2010 (*WW*). One March 6, 2010 (*CSi*). One February 3, 2011 (*WW*).

DOWNY WOODPECKER Common resident and breeder.

HAIRY WOODPECKER Rare visitor. One calling (*HL*).

NORTHERN FLICKER Common resident and breeder. Occasionally, a yellow-shafted appears and contributes to the gene pool.

PILEATED WOODPECKER Rare visitor. One May 30 and 31, 2000 (*Tw/DWP*). Two July 14, 2002; one November 9, 2003 (*CSi*). One March 4, 2007 (*BtW*, *EvH*). One April 5 and 21, 2009 (*EvH*). One April 25, 2009 (*CSi*, *KAS*). One December 2, 2009 (*CSi*). One April 1, 2011 (*EvH*). One May 4, 2011 (*CSi*).

OLIVE-SIDED FLYCATCHER Rare visitor. One May 20, 1981 (*ER*). One August 27, 2003 (*WOS/TAv*.) One August 29, 2008 (*CSi*). One August 10, 2009 (*JeB*, *CSi*). One August 30, 2010; one May 12, 2011 (*CSi*). One May 13, 2011 (*KS*, *CZ*).

WESTERN WOOD-PEWEE Regular migrant. Possible breeder, 2010, 2011 (*CSi*).

White-crowned Sparrow © Doug Parrott

WILLOW FLYCATCHER Common summer breeder in 1940s (*HL*). Now usually a visitor, most common in fall migration. However, singing males present in summer 2009, 2010, 2011 (*CSi, EvH*).

LEAST FLYCATCHER Rare visitor. One August 17, 1998 (*WOS/KA*).

DUSKY FLYCATCHER Rare visitor. One May 17, 2011 (*CSi*).

HAMMOND'S FLYCATCHER Uncommon migrant; usually one present each spring. Most recent sightings: May 2, 3, and 4, 2011 (*CSi*).

GRAY FLYCATCHER Rare visitor. One August 27, 2004 (*WOS/SMa*).

PACIFIC-SLOPE FLYCATCHER Uncommon migrant.

SAY'S PHOEBE Uncommon early spring or fall migrant; usually one present briefly each year.

ASH-THROATED FLYCATCHER Rare visitor. One August 31, 1975 (*EH*). One August 31, 2009 (*CSi, KL*).

TROPICAL KINGBIRD Rare visitor. One October 27, 2007 (*WOS/EH*).

WESTERN KINGBIRD Uncommon spring or fall visitor. Most recent sightings: Three April 22, 2009, two staying for several days (*CSi, KAS*). One May 13, 2009, remaining for at least two days (*DPa, CSi*). One August 19, 2009 (*MBJ*). One June 8, 2010 (*Many observers*). One May 9, 2011 (*JW*). One May 29, 2011 (*AK*).

EASTERN KINGBIRD Rare visitor. One June 17 and 25, 1982; one July 6, 1982 (*ER*). One June 12, 1994 (*CPe*). One June 15, 1996 (*WOS/RR*). One August 9, 1997 (*WOS/TAv*). One June 7, 1998 (*WOS/BB*). One July 18, 1999 (*WOS/TAv*). One August 1, 1999 (*WOS/ST*). One May 29, 2005 (*WOS/TAv*.) One June 10, 2005 (*WOS/LrB*). Two June 19, 2005 (*WOS/DoM*). One May 29, 2006 (*CSi, MtB*). One June 12, 2011 (*CSi*).

SCISSOR-TAILED FLYCATCHER Rare visitor. One August 2, 2003 (*WOS/SMa, CrM*).

LOGGERHEAD SHRIKE Rare visitor. One May 25, 1975 (*DP*). One April 10, 1989 (*KA*). One March 31, 2004 (*WOS/DMv*). One April 12, 2008; one March 4 and 5, 2009; one April 5, 2011 (*CSi*).

NORTHERN SHRIKE Occurred regularly in October in the 1970s and 1980s (*KA*). Now uncommon fall visitor; usually one present each year. Most recent sightings: One November 14, 2008 (*CSi*). One (possibly two) October 10, 11, and 25, 2009 and again November 4, 2009 (*CSi, EvH, JT*). One October 6, 2010 (*EvH*).

CASSIN'S VIREO Rare migrant. One May 1, 1981 (*ER*). One June 18, 1987 (*KA*). Flock on September 3, 2003; one September 5, 2004; one September 3, 2008; one May 23, 2009; one September 10, 2010; one May 12, 2011 (*CSi*).

BLUE-HEADED VIREO Rare migrant. One September 8, 1995 (*WOS/KA*).

HUTTON'S VIREO Rare visitor. One April 15 and 19, 2007 (*BtW*). One October 28, 2008 (*KL*). One May 1, 2011 (*IU*).

WARBLING VIREO Regular migrant in spring and fall in small numbers.

RED-EYED VIREO Rare migrant. Four August 19, 1995 (*WOS/RR*). Two August 24, 1995 (*WOS/DB*). One August 22 and 29, 1996 (*WOS/KA*). One May 17, 2008; one September 2, 2009 (*CSi*). One September 9, 2010; three September 10, 2010 (*KAS*).

STELLER'S JAY Common resident and breeder, reliably found in Yesler Swamp.

WESTERN SCRUB-JAY Rare visitor. One September 24,1998 (*WOS/TAv*). One October 8, 2005 (*Tw/JBr*). One September 26, 2008, observed for a few days (*CSi*). One September 21, 2009, staying through the winter (*KG, CSi*). One October 1, 2010; joined by as many as six until May 6, 2011 (*CSi, and many observers*).

AMERICAN CROW Common resident. Bred near kiosk, spring 2011 (*CSi*).

COMMON RAVEN Rare visitor. One March 11, 2009 (*CSi*).

HORNED LARK Scarce migrant (usually very late fall), seen one or two dates each year up to 2000s. Now rare. Most recent sightings: one December 4 and 5, 2005 (*MtB; WOS/TAv, JB, MiH*). One September 12, 2009 (*CSi, TK*).

PURPLE MARTIN Common summer visitor and fall migrant in the 1940s (*HL*) up to the 1970s (*KA*). Now uncommon migrant. Most recent sightings: One August 12, 2009 (*EvH*, *GTh*, *CSi*); two seen later that day (*EvH*). One August 20, 2009 (*AdS*). One June 6, 2010; four September 7, 2010; six September 21, 2010; 30 or more August 16, 2011 (*CSi*).

TREE SWALLOW Common summer resident and breeder.

VIOLET-GREEN SWALLOW Common summer resident and breeder.

NORTHERN ROUGH-WINGED SWALLOW Uncommon migrant; a few seen every year.

BANK SWALLOW Rare migrant. One May 30 through June 4, 1980; one September 4, 1980; one April 24, 1981 (*ER*). One August 21 and September 1, 1993 (*WOS/RTh*). One May 12, 1998 (*WOS/BB*). One August 9, 2003 (*WOS/SMa*). One May 11, 2004 (*WOS/SMa*). One August 27, 2004; one March 19, 2008; three August 3, 2010 (*CSi*).

CLIFF SWALLOW Common summer resident and breeder.

BARN SWALLOW Common summer resident and breeder; occasionally present in other seasons, though not as year-round resident.

BLACK-CAPPED CHICKADEE Common resident and breeder.

CHESTNUT-BACKED CHICKADEE Uncommon visitor. Most recent sightings: One March 6, 2009; one October 6, 2010 (*EvH*). One February 21, 2011 (*SR*). Two July 9, 2011 (*EvH*).

BUSHTIT Common resident and breeder.

RED-BREASTED NUTHATCH Uncommon visitor; when seen, usually in Surber Grove. Most recent sightings: One August 23, 2009; one August 30 and 23, 2010 (*CSi*). One September 2, 2010 (*EvH*). One April 23, 2011; one May 6, 2011 (*KAS*). One August 4, 2011 (*CSi*).

BROWN CREEPER Uncommon resident and breeder.

BEWICK'S WREN Common resident and breeder.

HOUSE WREN Rare visitor. One August 7, 2004; one August 18, 2007; one May 9, 2009; one August 25, 2010 (*CSi*).

PACIFIC WREN Uncommon winter resident; most often found in Yesler Swamp and along the treeline in Sidles Swamp.

MARSH WREN Common resident and breeder.

GOLDEN-CROWNED KINGLET Uncommon visitor, most often seen in winter and during migration.

RUBY-CROWNED KINGLET Common winter resident.

MOUNTAIN BLUEBIRD Rare visitor. One October 18,1984 (*ER*). One May 14, 1994 (*WOS/TP*). One September 28, 2007 (*WOS/MkW*). Two females April 3, 2009 (*CSi*). One female April 12, 2010 (*CSi*).

SWAINSON'S THRUSH Uncommon summer resident in the 1940s (*HL*). Recorded most years in the 1970s and 1980s (*KA*). Now uncommon migrant. Most recent sightings: One April 7, 2009 (*CSi*, *EvH*). Two April 25, 2009 (*KAS*). One May 15, 2010 (*CSi*). One September 2, 2010 (*EvH*). One May 22, 2011 (*CSi*).

HERMIT THRUSH Uncommon migrant and winter resident. Most recent sightings: Two April 24, 2009 (*CSi*). Two April 25, 2009 (*CSi*, *KAS*). One October 22, 2009; one December 7, 2009; one April 26, 2010 (*CSi*). One November 24, 2010 (*EvH*). One April 21, 2011 (*CSi*).

AMERICAN ROBIN Common resident and breeder.

VARIED THRUSH Uncommon visitor. Most recent sightings: One April 18, 2009; one September 22, 2010 (*CSi*). Two December 4, 2010 (*EvH*). Two January 1, 2011 (*CSi*). One February 26, 2011 (*EvH*).

NORTHERN MOCKINGBIRD Rare visitor. One October 28, 1993 (*WOS/KA*, *DB*).

BROWN THRASHER Rare visitor. One June 12, 2011 (*CSi*).

SAGE THRASHER Rare visitor. One May 11 through 24, 2002 (*WOS/DP*, *CSi*).

EUROPEAN STARLING Common resident and breeder.

AMERICAN PIPIT Uncommon visitor. Most common in September, October, April, and May; sometimes overwinters. High count: more than 60, September 16, 2006 (*CSi*).

CEDAR WAXWING Common when fruit is available; nested in 2008 (*CSi*).

TENNESSEE WARBLER   Rare migrant. One September 8, 1995 (*WOS/KA*) and again September 9 (*WOS/GT*). One August 19, 2009 (*CSi*).

ORANGE-CROWNED WARBLER   Common migrant.

NASHVILLE WARBLER   Rare migrant. One September 10, 1985 (*KA*). One September 25, 1994 (*WOS/DMc*). One September 10, 2005 (*WOS/TKL*). One September 30, 2005 (*WOS/KA*). One April 28, 2007; one April 26, 2008 (*CSi*). One May 10, 2008 (*EvH*). One May 12, 2008; one August 22, 2008 (*MtB*). One April 24, 2009 (*CSi*). One May 9, 2009 (*Seattle Audubon Board Birdathon*). One May 12, 2011 (*PK*).

YELLOW WARBLER   Common migrant and occasional breeder.

YELLOW-RUMPED WARBLER   Common migrant and winter resident. Both forms, Myrtle and Audubon's, are present.

BLACK-THROATED GRAY WARBLER   Uncommon migrant. Usually at least one or two found each spring and fall. Unusually high numbers of individuals mid-August 2009 (*JeB, EvH, CSi*).

TOWNSEND'S WARBLER   Uncommon migrant. Most recent sighting: at least three males and one female May 22, 2011 (*CSi*).

PALM WARBLER   Rare visitor. One September 13 to 17, 1993 (*WOS/EN*). One September 20, 1998 (*WOS/BB*). One December 30, 2000 through April 15, 2001 (*WOS/RL and many observers*).

AMERICAN REDSTART   Rare migrant. One August 26, 1988 (*KA*).

NORTHERN WATERTHRUSH   Rare migrant. One August 17, 1989 (*KA*). One August 30, 1998 (*WOS/BV*). One August 21, 2003 (*WOS/TAv*).

MACGILLIVRAY'S WARBLER   Rare migrant. One September 21, 1980; one April 30, 1981; one May 3, 1981; one May 18, 1982 (*ER*). One September 10, 1985; one August 16, 1989; one August 24, 1989 (*KA*). One August 24, 1995 (*WOS/DB*). One August 18, 1998 (*WOS/TAv*). One September 1998 (*BV*). One August 15, 2004 (*WOS/TAv*). One May 21 and 30, 2008; one June 4, 2008; one August 12, 2008 (*MtB*). One August 19, 2009 (*CSi, JeB*). One August 15, 2010; one August 10, 2011 (*CSi*).

COMMON YELLOWTHROAT   Common summer resident and breeder.

WILSON'S WARBLER   Common migrant.

WESTERN TANAGER   Uncommon spring and fall migrant.

SPOTTED TOWHEE   Common resident and breeder.

AMERICAN TREE SPARROW   Rare winter visitor. One January 11 and 15, 1981; one October 15 and November 7, 1981 (*ER*). One October 21, 1993 (*WOS/RTh*). One October 24, 2008; one February 21, 2009 (*CSi*). Formerly more common, averaging one or two a year (*KA*).

CHIPPING SPARROW   Uncommon visitor. Most recent sightings: One April 28, 2007; three July 24, 2007 (*CSi*). One August 20, 2007 (*MtB*). One October 2, 2007; one November 18, 2007 (*BtW*). One August 3, 2008 (*CSi*). One April 7, 2009 (*EvH*). One April 14, 2009; one June 5, 2011 (*CSi*).

CLAY-COLORED SPARROW   Rare visitor. One November 7, 1999 (*CSi*). One April 28, 2008 (*MtB*). One September 5 and 6, 2008 (*WOS/JeB; CSi*).

BREWER'S SPARROW   Rare visitor. One April 27, 1995 (*WOS/CH*). One September 22, 1998 (*WOS/TAv*).

VESPER SPARROW   Rare visitor. One April 18, 1973 (*FK*). One May 8, 1976 (*KA*). One September 23 and 29, 1981 (*ER*). One September 5 to 12, 1985; one September 11, 1986 (*KA*). One April 29, 1996 (*WOS/MS*). One April 21, 1998 (*WOS/BB*). One September 24, 2002 (*WOS/MiH*). One September 1 to 10, 2005 (*WOS/KA, TKL*). One September 9, 2008; one April 5, 2009 (*CSi*). One September 2, 2010 (*RL*). One September 12, 2010 (*CSi*).

LARK SPARROW   Rare visitor. One August 12, 2007 (*CSi*).

BLACK-THROATED SPARROW   Rare visitor. One May 19, 1989 (*KA*).

SAGE SPARROW   Rare visitor. One February 17 to 19, 1980 (*EH*).

SAVANNAH SPARROW   Common summer resident and breeder.

FOX SPARROW   Uncommon winter resident.

SONG SPARROW   Common resident and breeder.

LINCOLN'S SPARROW   Common winter resident.

SWAMP SPARROW   Rare visitor. One November 20, 1987 (*KA*). One seen frequently from November 20 through December 24, 1995 (*WOS/DMc*). One April 14, 1996 (*WOS/DMc*). One April 5, 2005 (*WOS/ST, DnF*). One seen frequently in April 2008 (*CSi*).

WHITE-THROATED SPARROW   Rare visitor. One October 4, 1981 (*ER*). One October 26, 1984 (*KA*). One October 7, 1993 (*WOS/RR*). One September 30, 1998 (*WOS/Tw*). One October 26, 2003 (*CSi*). One March 19, 2007 (*MtB*). One April 18 and 19, 2009 (*CSi*). One January 3 and 7, 2010 (*VJK; EvH; CSi*). One January 25, 2011 (*CSi*).

HARRIS'S SPARROW   Rare visitor. One November 10, 1974 (*FK*). One November 1992 (*CSi*). One November 23 through December 18, 1993 (*WOS/LCo, RTh, DMc*).

WHITE-CROWNED SPARROW   Common resident and summer breeder (*pugetensis* subspecies more common; *gambelli* seen mostly in migration).

GOLDEN-CROWNED SPARROW   Common winter resident.

DARK-EYED JUNCO   Common winter resident, reliably found in Yesler Swamp.

LAPLAND LONGSPUR   Regular fall migrant in 1980s (*KA*). Most recent sighting: October 6 through 18, 2007 (*WOS/BtW, MiH, MtB, CSi*).

CHESTNUT-COLLARED LONGSPUR   Rare migrant. One December 3 through 12, 1995 (*MS, CSi, WOS/CM*).

SNOW BUNTING   Rare visitor. One November 1975; one February 1976 (*KA*).

ROSE-BREASTED GROSBEAK   Rare visitor. One June 1 and 3, 2003 (*WOS/RSh, MiD*).

BLACK-HEADED GROSBEAK   Uncommon migrant and sometime summer visitor.

LAZULI BUNTING   Rare visitor and breeder (evidence of breeding in 2008). One May 25, 1974 (*FK*). One June 29 and July 9, 1983 (*ER*). One August 19, 1988 (*KA*). One July 22, 1998 (*WOS/TAv*). One May 10, 2004 (*WOS/SMa*). One pair and possibly one other male, summer 2008; male first recorded June 1; immature recorded that year (*CSi, EvH*). Two males May 10, 2009 (*EvH*). A pair June 17, 2009 (*JeB*). One May 29, 2010 (*CSi*). Three June 7, 2010 (*EvH*).

INDIGO BUNTING   Rare visitor. One September 14, 1988 (*KA*).

BOBOLINK   Rare visitor. One May 25, 1979; one June 2 and 3, 1980; one May 28, 1981; one September 3 and 14, 1981 (*EH*). One August 15, 1982; one October 10, 1983 (*ER*). One October 1 and 2, 1995 (*DP; WOS/BSu*).

RED-WINGED BLACKBIRD   Common summer resident and breeder; also common as migrant.

WESTERN MEADOWLARK   Former common summer resident in the 1940s (*HL*), now regular visitor in spring and fall. Three overwintered in 2008 (*CSi*) and one in 2009 (*CSi*).

YELLOW-HEADED BLACKBIRD   Uncommon migrant. Most recent sightings: May 7, 2010; May 4, 2011 (*CSi*). One June 11, 2011 (*TK*).

RUSTY BLACKBIRD   Rare visitor. One October 5 through 8, 1993 (*WOS/EN, KA*). One September 24, 1994 (*WOS/EN*). One October 31 to November 5, 1995 (*WOS/KA, EN*).

BREWER'S BLACKBIRD   Common summer resident and breeder, with a colony in the bushes around the helipad.

BROWN-HEADED COWBIRD   Common summer resident and breeder.

BULLOCK'S ORIOLE   Uncommon summer visitor and occasional summer resident. One pair nested in 1986. Most recent sightings: One May 1, 2008 (*MtB*). One June 4, 2009 (*EvH*). One May 28, 2011 (*EvH*). One June 30, 2011 (*JZ*).

GRAY-CROWNED ROSY-FINCH   Rare visitor. Nine November 30, 1973 (*FK*).

PURPLE FINCH   Occasional visitor, most often in migration but sometimes in other seasons. Reported breeding, spring 2009 (*JeB*).

HOUSE FINCH Common resident and breeder.
RED CROSSBILL Rare visitor, usually flyover. One flock of fifteen May 2, 1985. Flock of eight, April 19, 2009 (*JeB*); five seen on same day (*KAS, HG, HN*). Large flock April 22, 2009 (*EvH, CSi*).
COMMON REDPOLL Rare winter visitor. A flock of 28 on February 3, 1982 (*ER*).
PINE SISKIN Uncommon visitor in spring, fall, and winter.
AMERICAN GOLDFINCH Common resident, less common as a breeder.
EVENING GROSBEAK Uncommon visitor, usually flyover. Most recent sightings: One May 23, 2009 (*CSi*). One October 17 and 31, 2010 (*EvH*).
HOUSE SPARROW Uncommon resident and breeder.

Observers
(listed alphabetically by last name)

KA Kevin Aanerud (note: most observations are from "Birds Observed at Montlake Fill, University of Washington Campus, Seattle, Washington, from 1972 to 1989" in *Washington Birds* 1: pp. 6-21, 1989; some observations are reports Kevin made to WOS since that date and are documented in WOS records); *KAn* Kathy Andrich; *TAv* Tom Aversa

JBr Jessie Barry; *MtB* Matt Bartels; *FB* Fred Bird; *BB* BirdBox (telephone hotline, published in *WOSNews)*; *TB* Thais Bock; *LrB* Lauren Braden; *JB* Jan Bragg; *JeB* Jeffrey Bryant; *DB* David Buckley; *CBB* Charlotte and Bill Byers

PCr Peter Carr; *LCo* Luke Cole; *CCx* Cameron Cox; *PC* Paul Cozens

ED Ed Deal; *MDo* Mike Donahue; *MiD* Michael Dossett; *MtD* Matt Dufort; *PD* Peter Dunwiddie

MEg Mark Egge

JiF Jim Flynn; *DnF* Dan Froehlich

HG Helen Gilbert; *KG* Ken Grant

PHa Pete Hammill; *JHe* John Hebert; *HL* Harry W. Higman and Earl J. Larrison from their book, *Union Bay: The Life of a City Marsh* (University of Washington Press: 1951); *CH* Chris Hill; *MiH* Michael Hobbs; *MaH* Marc Hoffman; *EvH* Evan Houston; *EH* Eugene (Gene) Hunn

MBJ Melinda and Bruce Jones

VJK Vicki and Jim King; *LKi* Lann Kittleson; *TKL* Tina Klein-Lebbink; *AK* A. Kopitov; *PK* Penny Koyama; *FK* Fayette Krause (from *Birds of the University of Washington Campus* by Fayette F. Krause (Seattle: Thomas Burke Memorial Washington State Museum, University of Washington, 1975); *TK* Tim Kuhn

NLr Norma Larson; *RL* Rachel Lawson; *KL* Kathrine Lloyd; *SLC* Simone Lupson-Cook

DMc Dan MacDougall-Treacy; *SMa* Stuart MacKay; *TM* Tom Mansfield; *DoM* Douglas Marshal; *MFM* MaryFrances Mathis; *CM* Chris McInerny (note: most observations are from "Shorebird Passage at the Montlake Fill, University of Washington, Seattle, 1996-1997," in *Washington Birds* 8:19-28 (2002). Some observations are reports Chris made to WOS and are documented in WOS records); *DMv* Don McVay; *RyM* Ryan Merrill; *CrM* Craig Miller; *MC*

Robert C. Miller and Elizabeth L. Curtis, "Birds of the University of Washington Campus," in *The Murrelet* 21:2, pp. 35-46 (May-August 1940)

HN Henry Noble; *EN* Erica Norwood

GOO Grace and Ollie Oliver

DPa Doug Parrott; *DP* Dennis Paulson; *CPe* C. Pearson; *TP* Ted Peterson; *JP* John Puschock

SR Scott Ramos; *ER* Ellen S. Rattosh (from "Birds of the Montlake Fill, Seattle, Washington (1979-1983)," in *Washington Birds* 4, December 1995, pp. 1-34); *RR* Russell Rogers

AdS Adam Sedgley; *RSh* Ryan Shaw; *CSi* Constance Sidles; *JAS* John Sidles; *KS* Kathy Slettebak; *KAS* Kathy and Arn Slettebak; *MS* Mike Smith; *RSt* Rose Stogsdill; *BSu* Bob Sundstrom

JT Jay Taylor; *MT* Martha Taylor; *ST* Sam Terry; *GTh* Gregg Thompson; *RTh* Rob Thorn; *GT* Greg Toffic; *JT* John Tubbs; *Tw* Tweeters

IU Idie Ulsh

BV Bob Vandenbosch; *MVe* Mark Vernon; *DVi* Dick Viet

WOS Washington Ornithological Society (in "Washington Field Notes," published in *WOS-News* each issue); *MkW* Mike West; *WW* Woody Wheeler; *JW* Jacqueline Williams; *DWP* Deborah Wisti-Peterson; *BtW* Brett Wolfe; *EW* Ed Woodruff

CZ Carleen Zimmerman; *JZ* Jim Zook

Index